Arbitration

Law, practice and precedents

Arbitration

Law, practice and precedents

JOHN F. PHILLIPS
CBE, DCL, QC, PPCIArb, PPCIS

ICSA Publishing
Cambridge

Published by ICSA Publishing Limited
Fitzwilliam House, 32 Trumpington Street
Cambridge CB2 1QY, England

First published 1988

British Library Cataloguing in Publication Data
Phillips, John F.
Arbitration: law, practice and precedents.
1. Great Britain. Arbitration. Law
I. Title
344.107'9

ISBN 0-902197-72-X

Designed by Geoff Green
Typeset by Goodfellow & Egan, Cambridge
Printed in Great Britain by A. Wheaton and Co. Ltd, Exeter

Contents

Preface

When first approached by the commissioning editor of ICSA Publishing Ltd – the 'publishing arm' of the Institute of Chartered Secretaries and Administrators – to produce yet another book on arbitration law and practice, I initially had conflicting thoughts. On the one hand I was keen to do something for the Institute and its membership, in recognition of the very considerable debt of gratitude I owe to the Institute for all that it has done for me in the course of my career; on the other, I felt that perhaps there were already enough books on the subject to guide and instruct those who were interested – pillars of wisdom like Russell, Mustill and Boyd, Redfern and Hunter, and Bernstein's *Compendium*. On reflection, however, there seemed to me, as a practising arbitrator of some years in commercial, medical and agricultural disputes, to be no practical manual which brought to the informed businessman an explanation of the real advantages – speed, economy, privacy – of arbitration, over litigation, as a means of resolving disputes.

The lawyer is well served by the important works of reference mentioned above, particularly if his object is to exploit to the full the opportunities of our adversarial system. But is there not a case for a book which, while explaining the merits of the arbitral process, tries to advance the cause of simplicity and to mitigate those aspects of procedure which, in our courts, and now so often before our arbitrators, enable those seeking to delay the day of judgment to do so by adopting interlocutory procedures and devices calculated to result in delay and increased cost?

This is the reason for the emphasis in this book upon the 'documents-only' procedure for the relatively minor claim, and, indeed, for the structure of the book itself. It is in three closely-linked parts. The first tells the story of arbitration and seeks to advise on law and procedure. The second gives the authority for the statements on law and practice made in the first part, and the third, instead of giving a list of forms without life, provides a case study of an actual arbitration in operation from start to finish. This, linked with the narrative in the first part, should give the non-lawyer a clear and graphic picture of the way in which arbitration works, and will provide the experienced lawyer and arbitrator with a convenient check-list.

In completing this book I record my grateful thanks to two of my colleagues in Chambers at 1 Verulam Buildings: Dr Mark Hoyle, FCIArb, for his advice and views on reading the manuscript; and Miss Raquel Agnello, who prepared the index and also advised on presentation. Particular gratitude is also due to Mrs Barbara Davidson, formerly my PA in another sphere, who not only undertook the typing and reproduction of the whole text, but also took the opportunity to edit the work, correcting slips and cross-references, as well as supervising the grammar and syntax.

Acknowledgments

We are grateful to the following for permission to reproduce copyright material:

United Nations Commission on International Trade Law for the *UNCITRAL Model Law on International Commercial Arbitration* and the *UNCITRAL Arbitration Rules*.

The Controller of Her Majesty's Stationery Office for the *Arbitration Act 1950* and the *Arbitration Act 1979* (Crown copyright).

The Chartered Institute of Arbitrators for the *Arbitration Rules of the Chartered Institute of Arbitrators (1988 edition)*.

The London Court of International Arbitration for the *Arbitration Rules of the London Court of International Arbitration (1985 edition)*.

The International Bar Association for the *International Bar Association Supplementary Rules on Evidence in International Commercial Arbitration (1983)*.

Part One · *Arbitration law and practice*

1 · *Introduction*

Document .

Seminar

This book is intended to provide a practical guide to arbitration, not only for chartered secretaries, but for all those who in the course of their business lives encounter problems and disputes mainly arising from contracts in which they, or their organisations or clients, are involved; and to show how arbitration may often provide a speedy, efficient, inexpensive and private means of settlement of such disputes.

In the United Kingdom there are, of course, in connection with national and international commercial contracts, well-understood and accepted areas firmly established as suitable for resolution of disputes by the arbitral process. These areas include maritime contracts, commodity transactions and financial services such as banking, broking and insurance; and we have in the United Kingdom witnessed in the last hundred years a resurgence of the methods adopted in earlier times for settlement of disputes in international trade between merchants from the main trading nations of the world, when England – indeed, London – became the centre for these merchants' courts.

This resurgence is largely due to the fact that our common law absorbed much of the mercantile law of nations, and that, through our Commercial Court, great efforts have been made to establish and develop principles in arbitration law and practice and to create a high reputation for independence, integrity, specialist expertise and fair dealing for arbitration in the United Kingdom. The consequence has been that many national and international contracts contain specific provision for reference to arbitration in the United Kingdom of disputes arising under the contract; so that in such cases the court will stay any litigation arising under the contract and refer the dispute for settlement by arbitration.

Today, however, the 'catchment area' for arbitration is growing ever more widely in the general field of social contact and contract. It is a platitude to observe that when anyone gets on a bus and pays his fare he is making a contract – as he is when he goes into any shop and makes a purchase. Whether he is buying a washing machine or a holiday or is having his vacuum cleaner, television set or motor car repaired or serviced, a member of our society in his dealings with others is making commercial contracts of quite substantial size and importance, at any rate to the individual concerned.

This society, engaged daily in millions of commercial transactions, has changed almost beyond recognition in the last sixty years. It was noticeable up to the 1920s that Parliament and the courts, in declaring and administering the law, were concerned primarily with broad general principles. Generally, the State had not intervened in seeking to regulate or protect the personal lives of its citizens. There were, of course, statutes passed for the protection of broad groups of what today we would call the disadvantaged. These groups would include the poor, the borrower, the worker, the tenant – generally people who were thought to be at an economic disadvantage and potentially subject to duress. In the nineteenth century legislation was introduced for the protection of these disadvantaged groups so that one saw the passing of the Safety in Mines Act, the Factories Act, the Moneylenders Act and so on; and this was continued well into the twentieth century with the protection afforded to the occupier of property by such measures as the Rent Restrictions Act. But still, generally, a contract meant what it said. In the case of the sale and purchase of goods and services the maxim still stood as *caveat emptor*: 'let the buyer beware'.

A radical transformation has been effected in our society since the 1920s and particularly in the course of the Second World War. This was partly due to an outstanding improvement in the level of general education, at any rate to the extent that people were enabled not only to understand their rights as contracting parties but also to have the ability vigorously to assert them. Some may feel that the pendulum swung a little too far in emphasising the rights rather than the correlative duties and obligations. Be that as it may, we had a population much more articulate and knowledgeable than existed before the war.

Two other forces were at work. One was the rise in consumerism, steadily developing in Western industrial nations; and the second was the reaction to the monopoly, whether State or private.

In this country the control, or attempted control, of monopolies and restrictive practices, the abolition of retail price maintenance and the support for competition, even to the extent of creating new offences of anti-competitive practices, all coincided with the greater understanding by the consumer of his legal rights and a greater determination to pursue them with vigour. This assertiveness on the part of the consumer was supplemented by the readiness of Parliament and Government not only to exercise surveillance of contracts, but also to make provision for the amendment of contracts, or even their discharge, if they were thought to be 'unfair'.

Thus today we have a situation in which thousands of people, buyers of goods and services, feel that they have not had their due and are determined to obtain it. Great problems arise both for the administration of justice and for commerce and industry generally. It is doubtful whether any attempt has ever been made to calculate the cost of these disputes – merely the material costs of correspondence, interviews, telephone conversations and office administration, without taking into account the bitterness generated by a failure to obtain a fair deal. This situation has social as well as legal and financial consequences.

Efforts have been made to deal with the situation by the establishment of Small Claims Courts. It has certainly not been proved that these can do the job satisfactorily – and it is clear that the administration of justice generally in the courts of the land would be completely choked and brought virtually to a standstill if court proceedings were the only means of settlement.

This is where arbitration has such an important role to play. It is a method of resolving disputes that provides finality, is demonstrably independent, professionally competent and fair, and is inexpensive and private – a method publicised through all the advice centres, such as the various consumers' associations, the local Offices of Fair Trading, the Law Centres, the Citizens' Advice Bureaux and so on. The representative organisations of trade and industry providing the goods and services must be convinced of two things. The first is that support for the arbitral method of resolving disputes will, in fact, save their industry a good deal of money, because the costs of arbitration will pale into insignificance beside the actual administrative costs of wrestling with interminable disputes. The second factor is the public image of the industry or trade and, indeed, of the individual manufacturers or traders involved.

With the encouragement of the Office of Fair Trading, many organisations and trade associations concerned with the provision of goods and services to the public have established Codes of Practice offering facilities for settling disputes by arbitration under schemes independently administered by the Chartered Institute of Arbitrators. Among such schemes are those operated by the Post Office, British Telecom, the motor trade and industry, and travel companies. Housebuilding is another important field for administered schemes of this kind, where the maximum cost falling on even an unsuccessful claimant is nominal.

These schemes must be distinguished from those in which an Ombudsman has been appointed. The Ombudsman may well provide a valuable service in investigating complaints and making recommendations. But he cannot and does not make final and binding decisions on matters in dispute. That is the role of the arbitrator in providing a public service in the peaceful and just resolution of disputes – even between governments. In Britain arbitration not only gives the commercial community the facilities and expertise it needs for the purpose; it contributes very significantly towards the export earnings of this country and is reflected, whether through legal and other fees or through the provision of services, in our invisibles which so regularly convert an adverse balance in our terms of trade in goods into a surplus.

2 · *Arbitration – its purpose, origin and development*

The purpose of arbitration

The essential characteristic of arbitration as a means of settling disputes is that it is consensual – dependent upon the agreement of the two or more parties to the dispute – whether arising *ad hoc* or out of a contract containing a clause referring disputes to arbitration. For arbitration to exist there must be three elements present:

1. A dispute between two or more parties.
2. Agreement between them (expressed in the original contract or at the time the dispute arose) to refer the dispute to arbitration for decision.
3. The fact that the parties are to be legally bound by that decision.

This third element constitutes the principal difference between arbitration on the one hand, and conciliation or mediation (and valuation or certification) on the other (see below). It also distinguishes the arbitrator from the Ombudsman (a name imported from Scandinavia) who was originally (in the United Kingdom) a Parliamentary or Local Government Commissioner for Administration, but now provides authoritative and influencial advice on consumer complaints in banking, insurance and other services. His advice may well be accepted by the person or organisation found by him to be at fault, but he cannot and does not make final and binding decisions on matters in dispute. The decision of the arbitrator, however, if properly taken, is enforceable as a judgment of the High Court.

Apart from direct negotiation between the parties for settlement of the dispute, there are methods other than arbitration used for the resolution of the differences, including conciliation and mediation. These terms are often used as if they represented precisely the same process, that is, a procedure under which a third party endeavours to bring together the parties in dispute and to assist them to reconcile their differences. This is done mainly by the conciliator ensuring that each party is fully informed of the true nature of the other party's (or parties') views, but the process may be taken further by the conciliator himself devising and suggesting the terms upon which the dispute should be resolved.

Conciliation is generally recognised as a valuable method of resolving disputes, not least in the United Kingdom, and has acquired in some jurisdictions an 'official' or statutory status, but the essential point is that the parties are not bound by any conclusion on the dispute independently reached by the third party – whereas in arbitration they are. It is perhaps unfortunate that the term 'arbitration' is used loosely, particularly in the United Kingdom, to refer to cases, notably in the field of industrial relations, where the conclusions are not, and are not intended by the parties to be, binding upon them. Valuable though proceedings of this kind may be in the field of industrial relations in order to improve harmony and stability, it is misleading to describe them as arbitration.

Parties may, of course, try conciliation or mediation before referring the dispute to arbitration; such a course, however – if the attempt does not succeed – is likely to postpone, and increase the costs of, a final settlement. This is because in principle the conciliator, who may well have become, in the course of his work, informed of confidential and privileged matters and of possible offers or concessions by any of the parties, should not thereafter act as arbitrator. This is a general, but not universally adopted, rule of law, embodied in arbitration rules applicable in Europe, but not necessarily in the Far East.

Again, there is often some confusion between arbitration and valuation or certification. Thus where the 'referee', to use a general term, is to form an opinion based on his own judgment and skill as a valuer, the truth is that the parties are not actually in dispute and so the conclusion prescribed by the 'referee' is not an award by an arbitrator but a conclusion reached by a valuer. Moreover, where, as sometimes happens, a contract contains provision that some action to be taken thereunder must be 'to the satisfaction of' a specified person who is to certify to that effect, there is again no dispute and the 'referee' has undertaken certification and not arbitration.

The origin and development of arbitration

Arbitration has a very long history. It has been said that arbitration was known in the Egyptian civilisation, but the evidence is not really very reliable until one comes to the Ptolemies in the three centuries before Christ – and, after all, they were Greeks. It is safer to rely upon the Romans as the *fons et origo* of this method of settling disputes; Horace,

Ovid and Tacitus all make references in their works to the arbiter. If we use the Roman Republic as a starting-point, we find that by 280 BC the principal magistrate was the praetor, who was charged with the responsibility of presiding over litigation. His services were available to plebeians as well as to patricians. At the beginning of his year of office the praetor issued an edict stating the rules that he proposed to follow in exercising his jurisdiction.

While the praetor did not directly alter the law, the way in which he exercised his power had a great influence on the law as it developed. He was not necessarily a lawyer and no praetor's edict bound his successor, so that changes occurred from year to year. He was a functionary, appointed to decide upon disputed issues, generally of fact, between Roman citizens, and he became known as the Praetor Urbanus. When, owing to the great development of trade in the Roman world, a considerable number of foreigners, particularly merchants, became resident in Rome, a second praetor – the Praetor Peregrinus – was appointed to take charge of all litigation in which foreigners were concerned. The strict Roman law applied only to Roman citizens, and so the Praetor Peregrinus issued an edict of his own which drew, not upon the Roman civil law, but upon what was known as the Ius Gentium, the so-called Law of Nations, which at that time was in fact a code of rules observed in their intercourse by the trading peoples of central Italy. As with all reforming systems, the praetor's edicts hardened into a rigid system embodied in the general law under Hadrian in about AD 125 by Julian, the most prominent jurist of his time. This was the Julian who made such a major contribution to the codifying of Roman law which was built up largely by the great jurisconsults in the first two centuries of the Roman Empire from Augustus, finally crystallising, in AD 534, in the authoritative publication of a code of Roman law with the Institutes and Digest of Justinian. These are still a source of authority for the Roman–Dutch system in South Africa, as well as providing the foundation of the law in Scotland and Sri Lanka and the civil codes of the Romance countries of Europe.

So much for the Roman origins. The picture was repeated in the Europe of the Middle Ages, including Britain. Once again the same phenomenon arises – merchants doing much of their business by travelling from country to country and arranging for their merchandise to be carried from place to place to be sold in the great fairs and markets of the civilised world. The fair held at Leipzig in modern times is a survival of these mercantile fairs. This method of transacting business gave the fairs – at any rate the more important ones – an international character and bestowed a degree of universality on the legal rules based on the custom of merchants. In particular, when disputes arose, the merchants had need of speedy justice according to their customs and practice. In the Star Chamber in England in 1475, the Chancellor said: 'This dispute is brought by an alien merchant who has come to conduct his case here, and he ought not to be held to await trial by twelve men and other solemnities of the law of the land but ought to be able to sue here from hour to hour and day to day for the speed of merchants.' For some two hundred years before, it had been recognised that 'pleas of merchandise are wont to be decided by the law merchant in the boroughs and fairs'. The law merchant was based upon the Ius Gentium, developed principally in the Mediterranean cities and especially in Italy; and in England it was administered in the Pie Powder Court (the Court of Pieds Poudres, or Court of Dusty Feet), the best record of which is still available in the Red Book of Bristol written in the fourteenth century. At that time the law merchant was beginning to fall into the hands of the royal courts, where the emphasis was still on speed, simplicity of procedure and privacy. But by the seventeenth century the courts had become too antiquated, too cumbersome and too ineffectual in process to be popular, although their death struggle, with the law merchant being absorbed into the common law of England under Lord Mansfield, continued far into the nineteenth century. Indeed, it is only within recent years that we have seen the winding-up of some courts using the old forms, such as the Tolzey Court of Bristol.

All this has a great deal of relevance to the jurisdiction of the present-day arbitrator. That jurisdiction must be based upon and derived from the needs of the commercial community just as was the case in Roman times and in medieval Europe.

3 · *Control by law of the arbitrator and arbitration*

The jurisdiction of the arbitrator

The jurisdiction of the arbitrator – that is to say, the scope of the matters with which he may be concerned – depends fundamentally upon the agreement of the parties subject only to the law, i.e. the substantive law which will generally, in relation to disputes arising from contracts, be the proper law of the contract – itself determined by the express or presumed intention of the parties. In a large number of international contracts, provision is made that their construction, interpretation and enforcement are based on English law: the reason for this is simply because of the international characteristics of the commercial law of England, which, as we have seen in Chapter 2, is based on the custom of merchants long before the English language became, as it remains today, the main lingua franca of international trade and commerce. Accordingly, in discussing jurisdiction, reference is primarily made to English law; and the first question that arises is whether the law imposes any limits on the jurisdiction of the arbitrator.

Jurisdiction will generally depend on the terms of the contract. But there are certain respects in which, whatever the terms of the agreement to refer differences to arbitration, the arbitrator cannot exercise jurisdiction. Thus he cannot deal with a question of criminal liability. Without going into unnecessary detail in this connection, quite clearly, if a crime is alleged, then the State has an overriding interest in the matter and the accused person has a right of public trial. But, of course, a single transaction may give rise to a claim for damages as well as to prosecution for a criminal offence; in such cases there seems to be no valid reason why the arbitrator should not deal with the claim for damages even though it is desirable that the prosecution should first be completed.

Accordingly, in dealing with a dispute arising from a contract, the first place in which to look for the purpose of determining jurisdiction must be the contract itself. If it is properly drawn, the arbitration clause will ensure that the jurisdiction of the arbitrator is based on the widest possible scope. Thus a common form of arbitration clause is:

'Any dispute or difference of any kind whatsoever which arises or occurs between the parties in relation to any thing or matter arising under out of or in connection with this agreement shall be referred to arbitration.'

The clause should then preferably go on to specify the rules under which the arbitration is to take place – for example, 'under the Rules of the London Court of International Arbitration' – as explained on page 18.

There have been many cases in which the jurisdiction has been restricted by the terms used in the arbitration clause in the contract. For example, a phrase such as 'all matters in the cause' has been interpreted to apply only to matters specifically pleaded; and 'all disputes arising out of the contract', while covering matters arising in contract, will not extend to cover matters arising in tort, for example from negligence.

But in this connection one always has to bear in mind that, while the arbitration clause in the contract is the first place to which one may look to determine the jurisdiction, the jurisdiction of the arbitrator can be extended by agreement of the parties when steps are taken to appoint him; or even when the parties are making their submissions. This is merely another illustration of the fact that, fundamentally, jurisdiction depends upon the agreement of the parties.

So, in a sentence, the jurisdiction of the arbitrator must depend directly on the agreement of the parties and their desire for settlement of disputes by that method, subject always to the law – and that generally means the proper law of the contract in issue, the substantive law applicable to the case. But regard must also be had to another system of law which may or may not be the same as the proper law of the contract. This is the *lex fori* – the law of the place where the arbitration is held and which largely governs the procedure to be followed in the arbitration and the powers which may be exercised by the arbitrator. Regard must also be had to the law of the place of enforcement of the arbitrator's award, which, to the successful party, is obviously a matter of crucial importance.

The powers of the arbitrator

In turning to discuss the powers of the arbitrator – as distinct from his jurisdiction – we shall take the example of an international arbitration conducted in England. Since the extent and scope of the arbitrator's powers will be directly affected by the *lex fori*, the procedure in this case will be governed with reference to English law.

In England, the arbitrator's powers will in part depend upon the Arbitration Acts 1950 to 1979 of the United Kingdom Parliament; and the first point to make clear in connection with judicial review of the arbitrator's award is that by s. 1(1) of the 1979 Act the jurisdiction that previously existed in the High Court to set aside or remit an award on the grounds of error of fact or law on the face of an award is abolished. In practice that power was rarely exercised and perhaps the principal – and desirable – consequence of the abolition of the power has been to encourage arbitrators more freely to give reasons on the face of the award, as nowadays they may be required to do at the instance of the parties.

Much has been said and written over the years concerning the necessity or desirability of reasons being stated. Under English law the arbitrator may be required (by the parties or by the court) to give reasons; many believe that in the public interest (in generating confidence in the arbitral system), as well as that of the parties, reasons should be given. But that does not mean that the arbitrator should attempt to ape, in preparing his award, the more involved and abstruse terms of a court judgment. On the contrary, it is of the essence of arbitration procedure that it should be simple and informal, and, if the arbitrator finds for the claimant because he believes his evidence rather than that of the respondent, it is neither necessary nor desirable that (if he is acting in good faith) he should shroud that simple statement in his award by a mass of verbiage designed, often unsuccessfully, to protect himself from criticism.

There also existed another form of judicial review – by case stated to the court under s. 21 of the Arbitration Act 1950. Under that provision an arbitrator could, and if directed by the High Court had to, state his award or part of that award or any question of law arising in the course of the reference in the form of a special case for the opinion of the High Court; and, although the terms of the section seemed to give discretion to the arbitrator and, indeed, to the High Court, the cases show pretty clearly that, if a point of law were involved in the case, the arbitrator was best advised to adopt the special case procedure. This system of appeal to the courts of the forum on a point of law arising out of the case fell into disrepute, because of the way in which the procedure was used by a losing party, largely to postpone the day of judgment! Having regard to the problems of inflation, unstable currencies and other economic phenomena which we have all experienced in recent years, the virtual abuse of the procedure by case stated became very serious.

There was also the question of a potential constitutional – or, indeed, national – objection to the possible submission of a case in which governments were involved to the court of another nation for settlement.

This is mentioned only to confirm and emphasise that this method of judicial review has also been abolished. There is still a possibility of appeal to the High Court under strict conditions on a question of law of general importance, but, as explained in more detail in Chapter 5 (page 32), any such possibility can be excluded by the agreement of the parties. In the case of a domestic arbitration, i.e. one where the parties, whether individuals or corporate bodies, are all domiciled within the jurisdiction of the English courts, the agreement to exclude appeal must, to be effective, be made after the arbitration has begun; and so also where the agreement on which the dispute arises is a 'special category or s. 4 (of the 1979 Act) contract', i.e. concerns shipping, insurance or certain commodity agreements. There again the exclusion may be effected by the parties' agreement after the arbitration has begun. But in all other cases the exclusion agreement may be embodied in the original contract before any thought of a dispute has arisen.

Statute law governing arbitration in the United Kingdom

The law generally governing an arbitration in England is provided by the Arbitration Acts 1950 to 1979 of which certain parts extend to Scotland and Northern Ireland. The main statutory direction is provided by s. 12 of the Arbitration Act 1950. There are other provisions of the 1950 Act which are in point such as s. 18, which deals with the taxation and settlement of costs, but powers which are ancillary to the conduct of the arbitration by the arbitrator are generally covered by s. 12. This provides in the first place that every arbitration agreement (subject always to no contrary intention being expressed) shall be deemed to contain a provision that the parties and all persons claiming through them shall: (i) submit to being examined on oath; (ii) produce all documents within their possession and power; and (iii) do all other things which the arbitrator may require. Thus the arbitrator has complete discretion in the way in which the proceedings shall be conducted, except – and this is a most important exception – to the extent that the parties have in fact agreed otherwise either in the arbitration agreement or in the terms of appointment before the arbitrator enters upon the reference.

Section 12 goes on to provide detailed guidance concerning evidence

S - Section

to be taken on oath or by affirmation and, indeed, enables subpoenas to be taken out to compel the production of documents or the appearance of witnesses. Generally under s. 12 provision is made outlining the power of the High Court to make orders in support of an arbitrator to cover situations where his powers are not sufficient.

This has also been dealt with by the Arbitration Act 1979, which, by s. 5, enables the arbitrator or either party to apply to the High Court for the arbitrator to be given extra powers up to and including the full powers of a High Court judge in interlocutory matters. This differs essentially from s. 12 of the 1950 Act in that under the new s. 5 the High Court has power to enlarge the arbitrator's own power to make orders and leaves him to make the orders himself. Under the old s. 12 the arbitrator's powers are not extended and the court must act for him.

The Arbitration Acts 1950 and 1979, fully annotated, are reproduced in Part Two (pages 59 *et seq.*). It will be seen at once that, if the arbitrator had to depend only on these statutes for detailed guidance on the conduct of arbitrations, he might be at a loss; but it is always possible – indeed, very desirable – that the parties will make their own rules for conduct of the case. A properly drawn arbitration clause in an agreement will contain reference to such rules, usually depending on the nature of the agreement; but if the clause is silent concerning the rules to be applied, or if the very agreement to refer the dispute to arbitration is made *ad hoc* (there being no such provision in the contract under which the dispute arose), the proper course is for the parties to agree on the rules to be applied, on the advice of the arbitrator, as soon as he is appointed.

Appointment of arbitrator by law

How is the arbitrator appointed? In just the same way as the 'properly drawn arbitration clause' mentioned above should refer to the rules under which the case is to be conducted, it should (either by reference to such rules or directly) specify the method of appointment, e.g. by nomination by the president of the professional or trade organisation concerned with the commercial service involved in the contract, or by the appropriate specialist arbitration organisation, national or international.

If, however, the arbitration clause is silent on the subject of appointment of arbitrator (or the decision of the parties to refer the dispute to arbitration is taken *ad hoc*), the parties could ask the court, i.e. the national court of the country in which the arbitration is to be held, to make the appointment. Clearly it is better for the parties to agree the method of appointment (which would probably be used by the court) by inviting the president of the most appropriate organisation by reference to the nature of the original contract (whether professional, commercial or specialist) to nominate the arbitrator.

The procedure on appointment of the arbitrator is dealt with in Chapter 4, but the important point to be noted here is that arbitration in London has survived from the Middle Ages and flourished notably in three main fields: maritime affairs, the construction industry and commodity transactions. Why? Because the arbitral tribunal, whether a sole arbitrator, a duet or a triumvirate, is expected to have – indeed, is chosen because it has – expert knowledge and experience of the trade or industry in which the dispute has arisen. So in a shipping arbitration you expect to see one or more members of the tribunal drawn from the shipping industry who are not lawyers – perhaps marine engineers, shipbrokers or marine insurance experts. Similarly, you would look to the commodity trade association to provide an expert in the commodity field concerned to act as arbitrator. Nowhere is this more obviously manifested than in disputes arising from construction industry contracts, national and international, where architects, surveyors and engineers are acting as arbitrators all over the world. The essential point is that, unlike the judge, the arbitrator is chosen not for his great knowledge and experience of the relevant law and practice, but primarily for his expert and specialist knowledge and experience of the trade or industry concerned. Yet all must also have knowledge and experience of the law and practice of arbitration; and so you see technical experts and legal experts virtually engaged in teaching each other. In this context it is important to remember the differences in procedures and practice that exist between systems of judicial administration in the civil law and the common law countries – between the Roman and English systems referred to earlier.

Differing judicial systems

In recent years there has been much discussion of the relative merits of the 'adversarial' system as practised in the United Kingdom and the 'inquisitorial' system as it functions on the Continent.

The adversarial system is deeply rooted in this country's history. Holdsworth says that by the fourteenth century judges had become 'mere passive agents – umpires – set there to see that the law was observed by both parties and that the final decision was arrived at and executed in accordance therewith'. That position exists to this day in civil actions, where judges are required to listen, to evaluate and to decide, leaving argument to the parties. Therefore it is left to the parties to choose and call their own expert witnesses, subject to examination, cross-examination and re-examination; to require that all documents that are relevant (and some that are not!) shall be read in full in court; and to employ all those interlocutory devices ostensibly designed to define and delimit the area of dispute between the parties, but so often used for the purpose of harassing and destroying the other party's case. So we have pleadings, further and better particulars, interrogatories, applications for security for costs, applications for dismissal of the action for want of prosecution, applications for judgment in default of delivery of defence and so on. This procedure may well be suitable for litigation, but is it appropriate for arbitration? It is true that under s. 12 of the 1950 Act arbitrators are empowered to conduct the examination and an obligation is placed on the parties to do all other things which the arbitrator may require. Here there was a hint that inquisitorial powers might be conferred upon and used by arbitrators, but as recently as the Bremer Vulkan case in 1980 Lord Roskill was able to say: '... an arbitrator or umpire who, in the absence of express agreement that he should do so, attempted to conduct an arbitration along inquisitorial lines might expose himself to criticism and possible removal'. So, in spite of efforts made to secure the agreement of the parties to adopt rules which would give the arbitrator greater authority to introduce and exercise inquisitional powers, we still see parties calling rival expert witnesses to give evidence before an arbitrator who has the same expertise and who may not, in the absence of the agreement of the parties, call an expert of his own.

By contrast, what has the inquisitorial system to offer? Perhaps the greatest advantage derives from the fact that the judge is a senior civil servant, and a great deal of the preparation for trial and decision is done by the judge himself calling and interrogating witnesses, appointing experts and studying all relevant documents before the trial. This is not to say that one would submit to or advocate the abandonment of the adversarial system in arbitration law and practice and substitution of the inquisitorial. On the contrary, if we are to make the best use of arbitration in this country as a form of public service, then the procedure to be adopted must seek to harmonise and reconcile the two procedural systems by incorporating the best features of each appropriate to this form of judicial process. Moves towards such a development are discussed in Chapter 6.

Rules governing the conduct of arbitration

We have seen that the skeleton framework of rules governing the conduct of arbitration in the United Kingdom is provided by statute, the Arbitration Acts 1950 to 1979 Part Two, but that it is desirable – indeed, virtually essential – that the detail shall be filled in by the adoption of rules prescribed by the arbitration clause in the agreement under which the dispute arose, or otherwise by agreement of the parties. For the assistance of the parties in this connection, organisations have been created in the course of the past century in the United Kingdom (and elsewhere in the world), some of a general character, i.e. concerned with arbitration generally, and others of a specialist character concerned with a particular profession or trade or the services provided by a branch of commerce, finance or industry.

Of the general class, the oldest in the United Kingdom, and perhaps in the world, is the London Court of International Arbitration (LCIA). The Court was first established in the City of London in 1892 as the London Chamber of Arbitration on the initiative of the City Corporation. It developed as a result of association with the London Chamber of Commerce (and Industry – as its title now includes) to form the London Court of Arbitration, and in partnership with the Chartered Institute of Arbitrators (see details below) in the 1970s to become, in 1985, the London Court of International Arbitration. The LCIA is a corporate body with its administration in London under its Director and Registrar at 30 – 32 St Mary Axe, London EC3; but it operates on a world-wide basis. One of the first acts of the LCIA in 1985 was to produce a code of international arbitration rules designed for operation in any country and under any legal system. These rules have commanded respect and support from international arbitration around the world, not least because the rules, and the surveillance of their operation, are the product of the Court Committee comprising experts in international arbitration from Europe, Asia and North America.

The rules of the LCIA, together with the form of arbitration clause recommended by the Court for inclusion in the contract are set out in Part Two (pages 100–106). As implied by the title of the Court and the content of the rules, they are intended for use in international arbitration (see Chapter 6).

The other main 'general' organisation in the United Kingdom concerned with arbitration is the Chartered Institute of Arbitrators. That Institute is a professional body founded in 1915 and granted a Royal Charter of Incorporation in 1979. Its main function is to train and establish standards of performance for arbitrators. Admission to membership (Associateship and Fellowship) is by a combination of examination and practical (professional) experience. The Institute is in a sense 'postgraduate', since its members are drawn from many disciplines, including the law, engineering, shipping, the construction industry, banking, insurance, accountancy, chartered secretaryship, and other financial and commercial services. Its membership is international, there being professional members in 75 countries.

The Institute operates from 75 Cannon Street, London EC4. Apart from the normal services provided by a professional body – conferences, courses, seminars, library, journal, research, advice and information – the Institute maintains a carefully selected panel of experienced, trained and qualified members who can (and do) provide service as arbitrators with the requisite legal, technical or professional knowledge to settle disputes of any size or complexity wherever they may occur. For this purpose the Institute has at 75 Cannon Street a complex set of court, witness and retiring rooms, as well as relevant services, including telex.

In the main, however, the arbitration service provided by the Institute is for domestic arbitrations – those between parties within the jurisdiction; and the rules promulgated by the Institute in 1988 reflect this emphasis – by contrast with the rules of the LCIA.

The rules of the Institute effective from 1st January 1988 are reproduced in Part Two (pages 94–99), together with suggested forms of clause for inclusion in the contract.

There are, of course, other organisations of a general character that provide arbitration service internationally, including the International Chamber of Commerce (ICC), which has its seat in Paris and which has established a Court of Arbitration. Under ICC rules the Court appoints the arbitral tribunal and determines the place where the arbitration is to be held. But the procedure to be followed and the administration of the arbitration are left to the agreement of the parties and the decision of the tribunal. The Court scrutinises (and may comment upon) awards and fixes the arbitrators' fees and its own administrative charges.

Perhaps, however, the most important international development of modern times has been the production by the United Nations Commission on International Trade Law (UNCITRAL) of (i) a Model Law on International Commercial Arbitration and (ii) the UNCITRAL Arbitration Rules with forms of appropriate arbitration clause. These are referred to in Chapter 6 where the Model Law is reproduced (pages 38–50). The Arbitration Rules are reproduced in Part Two (pages 109–115).

Trade associations and professional bodies

Reference should now be made to some of those specialist organisations that provide a service to particular sectors of international trade, industry and commerce. As already noted, London has for centuries provided a base for arbitration in maritime affairs: this is sponsored by the Baltic Exchange and Lloyd's. For more than 20 years, a very experienced and widely used service has been provided at the Baltic by the London Maritime Arbitrators' Association, which maintains a working panel of about 50 members, thoroughly experienced in their field, who in their arbitrations publish perhaps a thousand awards every year, nearly all of them international.

By contrast there is the 'quality' arbitration: the 'sniff, taste, touch' test applied by the expert, ranging from a small private — indeed, secret — meeting of disputants with an expert to interstate trade or commodity disputes. Generally, the trade or commodity association concerned will have its own (rather esoteric) arbitration procedures adhered to by its members, again ranging in character from the Eleusinian mysteries to the sophistication of a court of law. The Grain and Feed Trade Association (GAFTA) is an important and valuable source of advice on commodity arbitrations.

The construction industry has many sources of advice and assistance in the settlement of disputes, national and international, by arbitration. Thus the Royal Institute of British Architects, the Royal Institution of Chartered Surveyors and the Institution of Civil Engineers will provide a service nominating and appointing arbitrators — generally in association with the Chartered Institute of Arbitrators. The industry also has its own Society of Construction Arbitrators with headquarters at 7 Gray's Inn Square, Gray's Inn, London WC1.

Many other professional bodies, as part of their service to the profession which they represent, will appoint arbitrators for settlement of disputes arising between their members — such as the Institute of Chartered Accountants, the Law Society and many more. The important matter for those seeking help in settlement of an 'inter-professional' dispute is not only the choice of an expert as arbitrator in that dispute, but also adoption of a code of rules for the conduct of the arbitration thoroughly tested by experience; this is the reason for the adoption in practice generally of rules on the lines of those designed for national and international cases by the Chartered Institute of Arbitrators and the London Court of International Arbitration respectively, which are set out in Part Two (pages 93–108).

4 · *Procedure and practice in arbitration*

Appointment of arbitrator

Once it has been established that a dispute exists between two parties, generally arising from a contract, the first step is to secure the appointment of an arbitrator; and for that purpose resort must initially be made to the contract itself. A well-drawn contract that contemplates the solution of disputes by arbitration will normally have an arbitration clause. The terms of the clause are important – reference is made in Chapter 3 (page 12) to this – and the clause itself should go on to provide means of securing nomination or appointment of the arbitrator in default of agreement of the parties. If the clause is silent on this point, or does not exist, it is of course competent for the parties themselves to agree, *ad hoc*, not only to refer the dispute to arbitration but also on the appointment of the arbitral tribunal, as noted in Chapter 3 (page 11).

Many arbitration clauses, for example, in contracts in the construction industry, in shipping, in financial services – indeed, in professional partnerships – will specify the nominating authority which will act at the request of the parties; but increasingly since the 1960s clauses have specified the President of the Chartered Institute of Arbitrators, the specialist body in arbitration, maintaining panels of experienced and qualified arbitrators in virtually all fields of commerce, finance and industry. The Institute is, of course, not only able to nominate and appoint; it is also always available for advice and recommendation even where it is not the nominating authority. Indeed, the Institute is able to provide all the facilities and services for the arbitration if the parties and their advisers so desire. Similarly, as noted in Chapter 3, where the dispute is international, i.e. where one or both of the parties are outside the jurisdiction of the United Kingdom, the London Court of International Arbitration can and does provide all such facilities and services.

Reference has already been made in Chapter 3 to the fact that the 'tribunal' may be a single arbitrator, a duet or a triumvirate. Practice varies. In the shipping world it is customary for each party to appoint his 'own' arbitrator, with provision for the parties to appoint an umpire if they disagree. Similarly in international cases the practice will be for each party to nominate his own arbitrator with an agreed 'independent' chairman. But 'unless a contrary intention is expressed therein every arbitration agreement shall, if no other mode of reference be provided, be deemed to include a provision that the reference shall be to a single arbitrator' (Arbitration Act 1950, s. 6).

As for the tribunal itself, no particular form (unless the contract requires it) is necessary for the appointment, but, of course, the tribunal must be told of and accept the appointment, and both sides must be notified before the appointment takes effect. There are few disqualifications from acting as arbitrator – in fact they can be summed up by saying that the arbitrator must be free of any conflict of interest or bias.

Once the arbitrator has accepted appointment, if he has not already done so, he should call for and inspect the arbitration agreement to confirm the validity of his appointment by reference to any special qualifications required. He must also at this time (unless they are prescribed by the arbitration clause) decide upon the rules by which the arbitration is to be conducted. He must of course secure the agreement of the parties to the application of these rules, and, as already noted in Chapter 3, he may well invite the parties to agree upon the application of the rules of the Chartered Institute of Arbitrators (in UK cases) or the London Court of International Arbitration (in international cases). These have secured wide acceptance and adoption in contracts in many parts of the world; and, as explained in Chapter 3, they vest in the arbitrator power to do many things in the course of the arbitration procedure that otherwise the court would have to be asked to authorise. The arbitration procedure is now outlined, and reference should also be made, stage by stage, to the rules themselves which are reproduced in Part Two and to the precedents taken from an international case which appear in Part Three.

Preliminary meeting

While in the simplest cases a preliminary meeting can be avoided, leaving the matters in issue to be dealt with by correspondence, in all cases of substance, the first step is for the arbitrator to convene a preliminary meeting with the parties and/or their advisers. The purpose of the meeting is to ascertain in general terms the true nature of the dispute and to determine the best methods of clarifying, narrowing, defining and resolving it. While in most cases the issues will be of fact, issues of law will often arise. So at the preliminary meeting the arbitrator should determine, and issue directions upon, such matters as pleadings – the formal statements of case of the parties in dispute. He may also ascertain the plans of the parties as to legal advice and representation (solicitors and counsel), as to disclosure of documents, as to evidence and even as to contemplated place and time of hearing. It is at this meeting that the stage is set for the conduct of the arbitration.

The counterpart in litigation of the preliminary meeting in arbitration is the summons for directions, on the hearing of which directions are given for submission of formal pleadings, statement of claim, defence and counterclaim, and reply and defence to counterclaim. The summons for directions may be restored from time to time by either party seeking interlocutory orders – further and better particulars of a pleading, interrogatories, security for costs, and so on. In arbitration, although the procedure is less formal, a similar pattern exists.

Pleadings

Accordingly, the directions given by the arbitrator at the preliminary meeting (at which he will take account of the provisions of the rules adopted for the conduct of the case) will generally be of the following order:

1. Points of claim (i.e. statement of case) to be submitted by the claimant to the respondent and the arbitrator within 30 days. The statement must set out in sufficient detail the facts and contentions of law on which the claimant relies, and the relief which he seeks. The statement should be accompanied by copies of essential documents, e.g. the original agreement, which the claimant puts forward in support of his case. (A specimen form of statement of case appears in Part Three (page 133).)

2. Points (i.e. statement) of defence to be submitted to the arbitrator and the claimant within 30 days of receipt of the statement of case, and similarly set out and accompanied as the statement of case. If there is a counterclaim by the respondent, it must be submitted with the statement of defence. (See the specimen statement of defence in Part Three (page 141).)

3. If a reply is called for, as a defence to counterclaim or otherwise, the reply is to be submitted within a further 30 days of receipt of the defence and counterclaim.

It is important to note that whenever a party submits a pleading, an application or even a letter to the arbitrator he must send a copy to the other side at the same time; and the arbitrator, in issuing directions or answering applications or letters, will send his response to both parties at the same time.

Although at the preliminary meeting there will be, as noted above, discussion of other matters relative to the conduct of the arbitration (discovery, legal representation, form of evidence, place and time of trial), those matters will probably not be the subject of formal directions at this stage. The directions issued will be generally confined to pleadings, leaving the parties to apply after close of pleadings for further directions. The directions themselves will be embodied in an order or letter issued by the arbitrator to the parties. (See specimen orders of directions in Part Three (page 144).)

Discovery and evidence

Discovery, of course, relates to the disclosure, inspection and supply of copies of all documents and correspondence relevant to the dispute and in the possession of the parties that are not privileged (e.g. letters between solicitor and his client). In arbitration discovery is dealt with by exchange of lists (not affidavits) of documents. The object is to produce, as a result of exchange and inspection, an agreed bundle, properly paged, for reference at the hearing by the arbitrator and the parties.

It is at this stage, following close of pleadings, that interlocutory applications may be made to the arbitrator; i.e. he is asked to revive the preliminary meeting to hear an application and give further directions. This may be a request for 'further and better particulars' of one of the pleadings, so that the applicant will be better informed of the precise case against him. Similarly, an application may be made for leave to administer interrogatories – a series of questions designed ostensibly to elicit clarity, but often used to 'fish' for evidence adverse to the applicant.

Under the rules mentioned earlier in the chapter, the arbitrator will have the power to adjudicate on such interlocutory applications, including applications to amend pleadings or for security for costs.

As to evidence, the arbitrator may direct that witnesses must attend to give evidence, orally, on oath or by affirmation at the hearing. But he may direct the parties to submit written statements (for exchange) whether or not verified by oath or affirmation; and the arbitrator will often find it useful and expeditious to direct that evidence on particular issues be given by affidavit in the first instance, reserving to the other party (and himself) the right to require the attendance of the witness at the hearing for cross-examination.

In dealing with all applications for further directions after the preliminary meeting, the arbitrator should give his ruling on the costs of the application and grant liberty to apply, i.e. to come back for further directions, if necessary. On costs, the arbitrator will generally decree and record that the costs of the application are to be costs in the cause (or reference); but, if the application is caused by the conduct (e.g. dilatory action) of one of the parties, the arbitrator may decide that the costs of the application shall be payable by that party in any event.

Finally, before turning to the hearing, reference must be made to the expert witness, who figures so largely in disputes in the construction industry. It should be remembered at the outset that the arbitrator in such disputes may well have been chosen for his professional experience and expertise in the section of the industry in which the dispute arose; and that he has, under the law and under the rules mentioned earlier, the right to appoint one or more advisers or experts on any matter to assist him in the conduct of the arbitration. But the parties may wish to call expert witnesses of their own. The number of such witnesses may and will be limited by direction of the arbitrator. Where an expert witness is called by one of the parties, special rules apply to that witness. He is, for instance, entitled to express an opinion – so long as that does not attempt to settle the issue before the arbitrator, who alone can do that – and may have with him when giving evidence the expert report that he has prepared. The expert, though called by one party, should preserve an independent role; he is not an advocate and should leave it to the party calling him to elicit the points to be made on that party's behalf.

Under the Civil Evidence Act 1972 and the rules made thereunder, unless the arbitrator gives leave, no expert evidence may be given at the hearing unless the party seeking to adduce it has applied to the arbitrator to determine whether a direction should be given for the substance of the evidence to be disclosed to the other party in the form of a written report. The basic idea of this provision is to ensure that each side is aware before the hearing of the substance of the other side's expert evidence, so that the area of conflict may be narrowed and both parties have time to deal with it at the hearing. The arbitrator has power to give such a direction and generally should do so.

The rules and practice relating to evidence by experts are generally the same for domestic as for international cases, but reference should be made in this connection to Chapter 6, where the UNCITRAL rules are explained and Part Two (pages 109–115) where they are reproduced.

The hearing

The date, time and place – and the estimated duration – of the hearing will be decided by the arbitrator in consultation with the parties, and on the application of one or both of them. It will normally be for the claimant's advisers to make the necessary bookings and reservations, the costs thereof being included in the claimant's costs of the reference. If a site inspection is required, the reservations may well include hotel accommodation bookings.

The hearing is private and only the arbitrator, the parties, and their advisers and witnesses are entitled to enter the room or court. With the consent of both parties and the arbitrator, others may be present during the hearing – clerks, pupils and so on. As for witnesses, if there are many, other than the parties themselves, it is appropriate that they should remain outside the room until called, but stay in thereafter if there is sufficient space.

The arbitrator, after making any necessary introductions and ensuring that only those entitled are present, will call upon the claimant or his advocate to open the case. The advocate will address the arbitrator, referring him to the matters in issue and outlining the way in which he proposes to establish his case – by argument and by evidence. After deploying any legal argument, he then calls his first witness. It is generally more satisfactory – if only to emphasise the serious and important nature of the occasion – that evidence should be given on oath or by affirmation, which the arbitrator has the power to administer.

At the close of the examination-in-chief, the giving of evidence at the request of the claimant's advocate, the witness is cross-examined by the respondent's advocate. While the law of evidence is not so strictly observed in arbitration as it is by the court, the arbitrator must be alert to the question of admissibility and be prepared to rule upon it. While, for example, leading questions are generally not permissible in examination-in-chief, they are in cross-examination.

On conclusion of cross-examination, re-examination of the witness by the claimant's advocate is permitted to allow clarification of matters raised during cross-examination.

When all the evidence for the claimant has been given, the respondent's advocate opens his case and follows a similar course to that described above; he then addresses the arbitrator, summing up his evidence and argument.

The claimant's advocate will then virtually conclude the hearing by exercising his right to reply. The arbitrator will not, of course, except in the simplest cases, make and publish his award at that time. He will take time to consider the evidence and arguments submitted and will notify the parties when the award is ready. But he may well invite the parties, before concluding the hearing, to address him on the subject of costs and perhaps also of interest if that is in issue, so that before reaching his decision he has heard all that the parties wish to say on the matter. He will then be in a position to make a final award.

5 · *The award*

Preparation and form of the award

The award of the arbitrator is the climax of the reference; its purpose is to inform the parties to the arbitration of the decision reached in such a way and form as to enable that decision to be enforced. Yet the law does not require that the award should be in any special form; indeed, it has been held that an oral award may be made, and, in the case of those commodity arbitrations where the case will be determined by 'sniff, taste, touch', an oral award may be effective.

But there are, of course, good practical reasons – not least the question of enforceability – for the award to be expressed in proper permanent form. Accordingly, it should be in writing and signed by the arbitrator, whose signature should be attested by a witness, for evidential purposes.

The award must be relevant to the issues at stake and complete and certain in its decision upon them. No expressions of opinion are appropriate; the award is a judgment, a decree, and should cover all matters in dispute.

In preparing his award the arbitrator must bear in mind that it will normally be intended to be the final judgment in the case, so that he should ensure that everything is covered, including interest and costs. Generally, there is no going back to the arbitrator after he has published a final award, since by doing so he is *functus officio*, and has no power to reopen the case; the only exceptions to this rule relate to costs, dealt with more fully below, and amendment under the 'slip rule', i.e. by s. 17 of the Arbitration Act 1950, which states: 'Unless a contrary intention is expressed in the arbitration agreement, the arbitrator . . . shall have power to correct in an award any clerical mistake or error arising from any accidental slip or omission.' (The Arbitration Acts 1950 and 1979 are reproduced, fully annotated, in Part Two on pages 61–92.)

There are many cases, however, in which finality cannot be achieved by the single award. Thus quantum of damages often cannot be assessed until issues of liability are determined: for example, where liability depends upon the true construction and interpretation of the agreement. In such cases it is appropriate and normal for the arbitrator to publish an interim award, as he has power to do under s. 14 of the 1950 Act. He must be careful to describe his award either in the title or in the text as 'interim', as otherwise, by virtue of s. 16 of the 1950 Act, it may be treated as final.

As to the form of the award, it should first record the parties by name with clarity and certainty. It should then contain sufficient recitals to make the award self-explanatory and complete, e.g. by a brief recital of the agreement under which the dispute arose, and the issues between the parties, the reference to arbitration and the appointment of the arbitrator. Then comes the operative part of the document – the arbitrator's findings and his award. The findings should set out the conclusions reached by the arbitrator, on the evidence and arguments submitted, on both law and fact, and then the decision is announced.

For many years there has been much discussion of the extent to which the arbitrator should give reasons in his award for the decisions reached by him. Initially, where the issue was a simple and single issue of fact, giving reasons for the decision was scarcely necessary, particularly where the arbitrator was appointed because of his experience and expertise in the matter in issue. There was also an almost inevitable tendency on the part of arbitrators to avoid stating reasons for their conclusions, at least in the award itself, if only to limit the opportunity of the unsuccessful party to challenge the conclusion. Under s. 21 of the 1950 Act, the arbitrator might be required to submit his award, or part of it, or any question of law arising in the course of the reference, in the form of a special case. This system of appeal was largely abused by losers seeking to postpone the day of judgment, and so was abolished in the case of arbitrations commenced on or after 1st August 1979. This was done by s. 1 of the 1979 Act, but that also provides that the court may order the arbitrator to state the reasons for his award in sufficient detail to enable the court, should an appeal be brought under the section, to consider any question of law arising out of the award. Accordingly, it may be positively concluded that the better practice is to state reasons; but this should be done simply, avoiding the temptation to introduce qualifications and provisos that tend to make the statement ambiguous or complicated.

A simple form of award, based upon the specimen pleadings there also set out – and included for the purpose of illustrating the principles outlined above – appears in Part Three (page 150).

The award takes effect on 'publication'. This is perhaps an unfortunate term, since the award is a private document and is not in fact 'published' except in the sense that it is transmitted to the parties.

What happens in practice is that the arbitrator notifies the parties, or rather their advisers, that the award is ready for collection or despatch on payment of his fees and expenses, as set out in an accompanying fee note or invoice. On either party paying that account, a signed copy of the award is delivered or sent to each party. The award itself will, of course, specify the party liable for those fees, and, if another has in fact paid them, that other will be declared by the award to be entitled to immediate reimbursement by the party liable.

Costs

The award should deal with the question of liability for payment of costs – both the costs of the reference, i.e. the costs incurred by each party to the proceedings, and the costs of the award, i.e. the arbitrator's fees and expenses. The arbitrator, by s. 18(1) of the 1950 Act, has full discretion to direct to and by whom and in what manner those costs shall be paid. But that discretion is a judicial discretion and must be exercised judicially in the same way as in the High Court.

That means that normally 'costs follow the event', and the arbitrator should direct that the successful party is also to receive his costs. But there are cases – for example, where a successful claimant has grossly inflated his claim and has been awarded much less than he claimed – when the arbitrator might reduce the amount of his costs payable by the other party.

What costs are awarded to the successful party? All the costs incurred by him, however extravagant he may have been in pursuing his claim? No. We have recently witnessed the passing of the classification of costs into solicitor and own client, solicitor and client, party and party, and common fund. Now the party awarded his costs will be entitled to his reasonable costs properly incurred as between opposing parties. By The Rules of the Supreme Court (Amendment) 1986 (SI 1986 No. 623(L2)), a new Order 62 (which deals with costs) was substituted for the Order 62 which had long subsisted. The new Order came into force on 28th April 1986 and provided new bases of taxation (i.e. assessment or moderation) of costs from that date. There are in fact two bases provided. The first – the standard basis – provides that on taxation of costs there shall be allowed a reasonable amount in respect of all costs reasonably incurred; the other basis is the indemnity basis, which provides for the allowance of all costs 'except insofar as they are of an unreasonable amount or have been unreasonably incurred'. The essential difference between the two bases is that, if the Taxing Master of the High Court has any doubts about 'reasonableness', those doubts in the case of the standard basis must be resolved in favour of the paying party; whereas in the case of the indemnity basis – typically as between the solicitor and his own client – any such doubts must be resolved in favour of the receiving party. The arbitrator, if he exercises his power to tax costs, will normally tax them on the standard basis.

The award will provide for taxation of the costs unless agreed. In fact the arbitrator has the power, under s. 18(2) of the 1950 Act, to undertake the taxation himself, but has been, until recently, disinclined to do so, preferring to leave that responsibility to be undertaken by the Taxing Masters of the High Court. Now, however, the Chartered Institute of Arbitrators provides a costs arbitration service, available to assist the arbitrator who conducts his own taxation, or the parties seeking advice on agreement.

As noted above, if the arbitrator has not made provision in the award for payment of costs, any party to the reference, within 14 days of publication of the award (extendible by the court), may apply to the arbitrator for an order directing by and to whom the costs are to be paid (1950 Act, s. 18(4)). The arbitrator must then, after hearing the parties, amend his award to deal with the costs.

The costs of interlocutory applications (leave to amend pleadings, security for costs, further and better particulars, etc.) must be mentioned. The arbitrator should, on each application, give directions as to the costs of the application. Generally, he will direct that they be 'costs in the cause', i.e. included in the final direction contained in the award; but, where the application is one occasioned by the dilatory or other unreasonable conduct of one of the parties, the arbitrator may direct that the costs of the application are to be borne by the defaulting party in any event; and the arbitrator must then remember to include the appropriate reference to those costs in his final award.

Interest

Where the arbitrator awards the payment of money, he also has power to award interest up to the date of the award on that money. This is not, of course, a penalty imposed on the unsuccessful party; it is simply proper commercial compensation for non-payment from the time when, as found by the arbitrator, the payment was due. While the arbitrator has a discretion, again it must be exercised judicially and the arbitrator should, in the absence of exceptional circumstances, so exercise that discretion as to require the losing party to pay interest, at commercial rates appropriate to the period of delay, to the successful party. That interest, as specified in the award, runs only to the date of the award. From that date interest accrues on the total amount payable by the award, as a judgment debt (1950 Act, s. 20).

Enforceability

Unlike a court judgment, an arbitrator's award cannot at once be enforced by levying execution. Indeed, until statutory provision to deal with the matter was made (by s. 12 of the Arbitration Act 1889) it was necessary to bring an 'action on the award', where the successful party to the arbitration had to sue, pleading and proving the arbitration agreement and award, and facing challenges to the arbitrator's jurisdiction and compliance with procedural requirements. Such an action is now rare in view of the procedure for enforcement available under s. 26 of the 1950 Act. This enables the successful party to 'register' the award by making an application under s. 26 to the court – even ex parte – supported by an affidavit exhibiting the originals or true copies of the agreement and award, whereupon an order is made enabling the award to be enforced as a judgment of the court. This procedure is not entirely a formality, but only in exceptional circumstances (e.g. where fraud is established) will the court refuse the order; it is particularly valuable where the award has to be enforced outside the jurisdiction.

Appeals

We have now to consider whether, and to what extent, appeal may lie from the award of the arbitrator. Generally this depends upon the system of law governing the arbitration in question; and the answer will vary according to the policy (as embodied in the law) of the State towards arbitration. Thus it is argued that it is unacceptable to parties who have, by their agreement, chosen to settle disputes arising therefrom by an arbitrator of their own choice to find that the arbitrator's decision may be set aside by decision of the national court, involving in any event unwanted publicity, delay and increased cost. On the other hand it is argued that a degree of judicial control of awards is desirable, not only to ensure that awards that are clearly 'wrong' in law are not enforced, but also to secure some degree of consistency of decision in similar cases.

English law changed drastically in 1979 in its attitude towards appeal from the arbitrator's award. Up to that time the High Court had the statutory power to set aside or remit (i.e. to the arbitrator for proper decision) an award on grounds of error of fact or law on the face of the award. As noted in Chapter 3 (page 11), that power was rarely exercised, and it was abolished by s. 1(1) of the 1979 Act. So also was abolished the judicial review of the arbitrator's award by case stated under s. 12 of the 1950 Act, which had fallen into disrepute for reasons explained in Chapter 3 (page 11).

English law has retained a right of appeal from the award of an arbitrator on a point of law (where, of course, the arbitration is subject to English law) by ss. 1 and 2 of the 1979 Act. However, this right of appeal is limited in that it requires either the consent of all the parties to the reference or leave of the court, which will be given only where the court considers that the determination of the question of law concerned could substantially affect the rights of one or more of the parties to the arbitration agreement.

The 1979 Act came into force on 1st August 1979 and applies to arbitrations commenced on or after that date, but in practice there have been few applications since then for leave to appeal, and fewer still that were successful.

The 1979 Act, however, also contained important provisions on the possibility of exclusion of that limited right of appeal by agreement of the parties; and in that connection drew a sharp distinction between the domestic and the international case. The effect of ss. 3 and 4 of the 1979 Act is that in a domestic case the right of appeal given by s. 1 cannot be waived or excluded by agreement of the parties *before* commencement of the arbitration – i.e. the exclusion may not effectively be included in the arbitration clause of the agreement – whereas generally in an international case it can. 'Generally', because there are exceptions explained below.

Therefore in an international case (subject to those exceptions) one can effectively exclude the right of appeal at any time before or after the commencement of the arbitration – by agreement of the parties, whether expressed in the arbitration clause or not – whereas in the domestic case such an exclusion agreement will be effective and enforced only if made, as is perhaps unlikely, *after* the commencement of the arbitration.

The exceptions mentioned above relate to international agreements in particular branches of commerce, as set out in s. 4 of the 1979 Act, namely Admiralty, commodity and insurance arbitrations. Although these are international cases, an exclusion agreement (of the right to appeal from the award) will not be valid and effective under English law unless made after commencement of the arbitration. It has been widely assumed that these special exceptions from the general rule now operative may, in the light of experience, be removed; but that could only be done by Parliament under the special provisions of s. 4(3) of the 1979 Act.

While not concerned with appeal from the award of the arbitrator, it is relevant to refer here to the possibility of removal of the arbitrator for good cause, e.g. fraud, bias, conflict of interest. This may be covered by the rules under which the arbitration is conducted – for example, Articles 3.7, 3.8 and 3.9 of the LCIA rules reproduced in Part Two (see page 100). But the High Court in England has jurisdiction to remove an arbitrator challenged for such a cause – see s. 24 of the 1950 Act.

6 · *International cases*

Special features

International cases, i.e. those in which either or both of the parties are out of the jurisdiction, have to be considered separately. As always, reference must first be made to the agreement under which the dispute has arisen. From this will be determined the proper law of the contract – the system of law which the parties to the agreement have agreed (or will be deemed to have agreed) will govern the interpretation and operation of the contract (see Chapter 3, page 11); and also whether disputes arising under it are to be settled by arbitration.

As already observed, arbitration is consensual, so that, if no provision is made in the original agreement for reference of disputes to arbitration, it is still possible for the parties to agree *ad hoc* to do so. The arbitration clause, if any, or the parties, may prescribe the rules under which the arbitration is to be conducted, whether in England or not, for example under the rules of the International Chamber of Commerce (ICC) in Paris, or of the London Court of International Arbitration (LCIA). As noted in Chapter 3, the modernisation in 1985 of the rules of the LCIA for world-wide use has secured the interest and support of the international community involved in arbitration. The rules are set out in Part Two on pages 100–108.

As mentioned in Chapter 4 (page 21), it is common in the case of international arbitrations for more than one arbitrator to be appointed – indeed, for each party to appoint his 'own'; and for a third to be agreed between them to act as chairman; or for an umpire to be called in, should the two arbitrators fail to agree.

However, perhaps the most important feature of an international arbitration conducted in the United Kingdom is that the right to appeal to the court from the award, limited as it is by the Arbitration Act 1979, may be excluded by the original arbitration agreement, or by the parties after the dispute has arisen. The relevant sections of the 1979 Act (ss. 3 and 4) have been fully explained in Chapter 5 (page 28), but the essential principle is as stated above and affords one more illustration of the consensual nature of arbitration. Indeed, it is (to those outside the jurisdiction) one of the attractive features of the English law of arbitration that parties, having chosen by agreement not only the system of law to govern the agreement but also the method of resolution of disputes arising under it, should not be compelled by what is to them a foreign national court to submit the result of their choice to the jurisdiction of that court.

United Nations Commission on International Trade Law (UNCITRAL)

No reference to international commercial arbitration would be complete without mentioning the work of UNCITRAL, set up in 1966 for the purpose of unifying the law relating to international trade, in effect recreating in a modern context the mercantile law of nations. Detailed reference to the work of UNCITRAL would be out of place in this book, but there are two projects of the Commission which are highly relevant.

The first is the production in 1976 of a set of arbitration rules. The availability of such rules for adoption in the case of *ad hoc* arbitrations is of the greatest importance, since they are so designed as to ensure the likelihood of international enforceability of the award. Such rules are not, of course, needed in domestic arbitrations conducted under the aegis of established institutions such as the Chartered Institute of Arbitrators or in international arbitrations under the rules of the LCIA or the ICC, since these rules have taken account of the changing and developing needs of the international trading community in the resolution of disputes. In *ad hoc* arbitrations, however, where no guidelines on procedure may be available, the UNCITRAL rules fill the gap. They are essentially rules of procedures, and not of substantive law, but they seek to serve disputants in both common law and civil law jurisdictions and under every system of government. The rules are accordingly reproduced in Part Two (pages 109–115), following those of the Chartered Institute of Arbitrators and the LCIA.

The other project of UNCITRAL which warrants special mention looks to the future – indeed, sets the stage for what may be the revolution of the 1990s in relation to arbitration law and practice. Entering upon the stage after years of discussion and negotiation between governments, the Model Law on International Commercial Arbitration was adopted by UNCITRAL on 21st June 1985. This Model Law does in fact, to a considerable extent, reconcile the procedures of the inquisitorial and adversarial systems and is now before governments for consideration. Note that it is a *Model* Law – unlike the directives under European Community legislation such as those designed to harmonise the company law of member states – and is there for adoption in whole or in part by the governments now confronted with it. Primarily it is, as its name indicates, a law for international commercial arbitration; but quite clearly it is desirable in our country, and probably in all, that there should not be substantial differences between the law for domestic arbitrations and that for arbitrations of an international character. It remains to be seen whether the Model Law is in fact adopted by the national legislation of many states, but as it may provide a glimpse of the future in international arbitration, at least in those states which do adopt it, the Model Law is reproduced in an Appendix to this chapter.

Appendix · UNCITRAL Model Law on International Commercial Arbitration

(as adopted by the United Nations Commission on International Trade Law on June 21, 1985)

CHAPTER I. GENERAL PROVISIONS

Article 1: Scope of application[1]

(1) This Law applies to international commercial[2] arbitration, subject to any agreement in force between this State and any other State or States.

(2) The provisions of this Law, except articles 8, 9, 35 and 36, apply only if the place of arbitration is in the territory of this State.

(3) An arbitration is international if:

(a) the parties to an arbitration agreement have, at the time of the conclusion of that agreement, their places of business in different States; or

(b) one of the following places is situated outside the State in which the parties have their places of business:

  (i) the place of arbitration if determined in, or pursuant to, the arbitration agreement:

  (ii) any place where a substantial part of the obligations of the commercial relationship is to be performed or the place with which the subject-matter of the dispute is most closely connected; or

(c) the parties have expressly agreed that the subject-matter of the arbitration agreement relates to more than one country.

(4) For the purposes of paragraph (3) of this article:

(a) if a party has more than one place of business, the place of business is that which has the closest relationship to the arbitration agreement;

---

[1] Article headings are for reference purposes only and are not to be used for purposes of interpretation.

[2] The term "commercial" should be given a wide interpretation so as to cover matters arising from all relationships of a commercial nature, whether contractual or not. Relationships of a commercial nature include, but are not limited to, the following transactions: any trade transaction for the supply or exchange of goods or services; distribution agreement; commercial representation or agency; factoring; leasing; construction of works; consulting; engineering; licensing; investment; financing; banking; insurance; exploitation agreement or concession; joint venture and other forms of industrial or business cooperation; carriage of goods or passengers by air, sea, rail or road.

(b) if a party does not have a place of business, reference is to be made to his habitual residence.

(5) This Law shall not affect any other law of this State by virtue of which certain disputes may not be submitted to arbitration or may be submitted to arbitration only according to provisions other than those of this Law.

Article 2: Definitions and rules of interpretation

For the purposes of this Law:

(a) "arbitration" means any arbitration whether or not administered by a permanent arbitral institution;
(b) "arbitral tribunal" means a sole arbitrator or a panel of arbitrators;
(c) "court" means a body or organ of the judicial system of a State;
(d) where a provision of this Law, except article 28, leaves the parties free to determine a certain issue, such freedom includes the right of the parties to authorize a third party, including an institution, to make that determination;
(e) where a provision of this Law refers to the fact that the parties have agreed or that they may agree or in any other way refers to an agreement of the parties, such agreement includes any arbitration rules referred to in that agreement;
(f) where a provision of this Law, other than in articles 25(a) and 32(2)(a), refers to a claim, it also applies to a counter-claim, and where it refers to a defence, it also applies to a defence to such counter-claim.

Article 3: Receipt of written communications

(1) Unless otherwise agreed by the parties:

(a) any written communication is deemed to have been received if it is delivered to the addressee personally or if it is delivered at his place of business, habitual residence or mailing address; if none of these can be found after making a reasonable inquiry, a written communication is deemed to have been received if it is sent to the addressee's last-known place of business, habitual residence or mailing address by registered letter or any other means which provides a record of the attempt to deliver it;
(b) the communication is deemed to have been received on the day it is so delivered.

(2) The provisions of this article do not apply to communications in court proceedings.

Article 4: Waiver of right to object

A party who knows that any provision of this Law from which the parties may derogate or any requirement under the arbitration agreement has not been complied with and yet proceeds with the arbitration without stating his objection to such non-compliance without undue delay or, if a time-limit is provided therefor, within such period of time, shall be deemed to have waived his right to object.

Article 5: Extent of court intervention

In matters governed by this Law, no court shall intervene except where so provided in this Law.

Article 6: Court or other authority for certain functions of arbitration assistance and supervision

The functions referred to in articles 11(3), 11(4), 13(3), 14, 16(3) and 34(2) shall be performed by . . . [Each State enacting this model law specifies the court, courts or, where referred to therein, other authority competent to perform these functions.]

CHAPTER II. ARBITRATION AGREEMENT

Article 7: Definition and form of arbitration agreement

(1) "Arbitration agreement" is an agreement by the parties to submit to arbitration all or certain disputes which have risen or which may arise between then in respect of a defined legal relationship, whether contractual or not. An arbitration agreement may be in the form of an arbitration clause in a contract or in the form of a separate agreement.

(2) The arbitration agreement shall be in writing. An agreement is in writing if it is contained in a document signed by the parties or in an exchange of letters, telex, telegrams or other means of telecommunication which provide a record of the agreement, or in an exchange of statements of claim and defence in which the existence of an agreement is alleged by one party and not denied by another. The reference in a contract to a document containing an arbitration clause constitutes an arbitration agreement provided that the contract is in writing and the reference is such as to make that clause part of the contract.

Article 8: Arbitration agreement and substantive claim before court

(1) A court before which an action is brought in a matter which is the subject of an arbitration agreement shall, if a party so requests not later than when submitting his first statement on the substance of the dispute, refer the parties to arbitration unless it finds that the agreement is null and void, inoperative or incapable of being performed.

(2) Where an action referred to in paragraph (1) of this article has been brought, arbitral proceedings may nevertheless be commenced or continued, and an award may be made, while the issue is pending before the court.

Article 9: Arbitration agreement and interim measures by court

It is not incompatible with an arbitration agreement for a party to request, before or during arbitral proceedings, from a court an interim measure of protection and for a court to grant such measure.

Article 10: Number of arbitrators

(1) The parties are free to determine the number of arbitrators.

(2) Failing such determination, the number of arbitrators shall be three.

Article 11: Appointment of arbitrators

(1) No person shall be precluded by reason of his nationality from acting as an arbitrator, unless otherwise agreed by the parties.

(2) The parties are free to agree on a procedure of appointing the arbitrator or arbitrators, subject to the provisions of paragraphs (4) and (5) of
this article.

(3) Failing such agreement,

(a) in an arbitration with three arbitrators, each party shall appoint
one arbitrator, and the two arbitrators thus appointed shall
appoint the third arbitrator; if a party fails to appoint the arbitrator within thirty days of receipt of a request to do so from the
other party, or if the two arbitrators fail to agree on the third arbitrator within thirty days of their appointment, the appointment
shall be made, upon request of a party, by the court or other authority specified in article 6;

(b) in an arbitration with a sole arbitrator, if the parties are unable to
agree on the arbitrator, he shall be appointed, upon request of a
party, by the court or other authority specified in article 6.

(4) Where, under an appointment procedure agreed upon by the parties,

(a) a party fails to act as required under such procedure, or

(b) the parties, or two arbitrators, are unable to reach an agreement
expected of them under such procedure, or

(c) a third party, including an institution, fails to perform any function
entrusted to it under such procedure,

any party may request the court or other authority specified in article 6 to
take the necessary measure, unless the agreement on the appointment
procedure provides other means for securing the appointment.

(5) A decision on a matter entrusted by paragraph (3) or (4) of this
article to the court or other authority specified in article 6 shall be subject
to no appeal. The court or other authority, in appointing an arbitrator,
shall have due regard to any qualifications required of the arbitrator by
the agreement of the parties and to such considerations as are likely to
secure the appointment of an independent and impartial arbitrator and,
in the case of sole or third arbitrator, shall take into account as well the
advisability of appointing an arbitrator of a nationality other than those of
the parties.

Article 12: Grounds for challenge

(1) When a person is approached in connection with his possible
appointment as an arbitrator, he shall disclose any circumstances likely to

give rise to justifiable doubts as to his impartiality or independence. An arbitrator, from the time of his appointment and throughout the arbitral proceedings, shall without delay disclose any such circumstances to the parties unless they have already been informed of them by him.

(2) An arbitrator may be challenged only if circumstances exist that give rise to justifiable doubts as to his impartiality or independence, or if he does not possess qualifications agreed to by the parties. A party may challenge an arbitrator appointed by him, or in whose appointment he has participated, only for reasons of which he becomes aware after the appointment has been made.

Article 13: Challenge procedure

(1) The parties are free to agree on a procedure for challenging an arbitrator, subject to the provisions of paragraph (3) of this article.

(2) Failing such agreement, a party who intends to challenge an arbitrator shall, within fifteen days after becoming aware of the constitution of the arbitral tribunal or after becoming aware of any circumstance referred to in article 12(2), send a written statement of the reasons for the challenge to the arbitral tribunal. Unless the challenged arbitrator withdraws from his office or the other party agrees to the challenge, the arbitral tribunal shall decide on the challenge.

(3) If a challenge under any procedure agreed upon by the parties or under the procedure of paragraph (2) of this article is not successful, the challenging party may request, within thirty days after having received notice of the decision rejecting the challenge, the court or other authority specified in article 6 to decide on the challenge, which decision shall be subject to no appeal, while such a request is pending, the arbitral tribunal, including the challenged arbitrator, may continue the arbitral proceedings and make an award.

Article 14: Failure or impossibility to act

(1) If an arbitrator becomes *de jure* or *de facto* unable to perform his functions or for other reasons fails to act without undue delay, his mandate terminates if he withdraws from his office or if the parties agree on the termination. Otherwise, if a controversy remains concerning any of these grounds, any party may request the court or other authority specified in article 6 to decide on the termination of the mandate, which decision shall be subject to no appeal.

(2) If, under this article or article 13(2), an arbitrator withdraws from his office or a party agrees to the termination of the mandate of an arbitrator, this does not imply acceptance of the validity of any ground referred to in this article or article 12(2).

Article 15: Appointment of substitute arbitrator

Where the mandate of an arbitrator terminates under article 13 or 14 or because of his withdrawal from office for any other reason or because of the revocation of his mandate by agreement of the parties or in any other case of termination of his mandate, a substitute arbitrator shall be appointed according to the rules that were applicable to the appointment of the arbitrator being replaced.

CHAPTER IV. JURISDICTION OF ARBITRAL TRIBUNAL

Article 16: Competence of arbitral tribunal to rule on its jurisdiction

(1) The arbitral tribunal may rule on its own jurisdiction, including any objections with respect to the existence or validity of the arbitration agreement. For that purpose, an arbitration clause which forms part of a contract shall be treated as an agreement independent of the other terms of the contract. A decision by the arbitral tribunal that the contract is null and void shall not entail *ipso jure* the invalidity of the arbitration clause.

(2) A plea that the arbitral tribunal does not have jurisdiction shall be raised not later than the submission of the statement of defence. A party is not precluded from raising such a plea by the fact that he has appointed, or participated in the appointment of, an arbitrator. A plea that the arbitral tribunal is exceeding the scope of its authority shall be raised as soon as the matter alleged to be beyond the scope of its authority is raised during the arbitral proceedings. The arbitral tribunal may, in either case, admit a later plea if it considers the delay justified.

(3) The arbitral tribunal may rule on a plea referred to in paragraph (2) of this article either as a preliminary question or in an award on the merits. If the arbitral tribunal rules as a preliminary question that it has jurisdiction, any party may request, within thirty days after having received notice of that ruling, the court specified in article 6 to decide the matter, which decision shall be subject to no appeal; while such a request is pending, the arbitral tribunal may continue the arbitral proceedings and make an award.

Article 17: Power of arbitral tribunal to order interim measures

Unless otherwise agreed by the parties, the arbitral tribunal may, at the request of a party, order any party to take such interim measure of protection as the arbitral tribunal may consider necessary in respect of the subject-matter of the dispute. The arbitral tribunal may require any party to provide appropriate security in connection with such measure.

CHAPTER V. CONDUCT OF ARBITRAL PROCEEDINGS

Article 18: Equal treatment of parties

The parties shall be treated with equality and each party shall be given a full opportunity of presenting his case.

Article 19: Determination of rules of procedure

(1) Subject to the provisions of this Law, the parties are free to agree on the procedure to be followed by the arbitral tribunal in conducting the proceedings.

(2) Failing such agreement, the arbitral tribunal may, subject to the provisions of this Law, conduct the arbitration in such manner as it considers appropriate. The power conferred upon the arbitral tribunal includes the power to determine the admissibility, relevance, materiality and weight of any evidence.

Article 20: Place of arbitration

(1) The parties are free to agree on the place of arbitration. Failing such agreement, the place of arbitration shall be determined by the arbitral tribunal having regard to the circumstances of the case, including the convenience of the parties.

(2) Notwithstanding the provisions of paragraph (1) of this article, the arbitral tribunal may, unless otherwise agreed by the parties, meet at any place it considers appropriate for consultation among its members, for hearing witnesses, experts or the parties, or for inspection of goods, other property or documents.

Article 21: Commencement of arbitral proceedings

Unless otherwise agreed by the parties, the arbitral proceedings in respect of a particular dispute commence on the date on which a request for that dispute to be referred to arbitration is received by the respondent.

Article 22: Language

(1) The parties are free to agree on the language or languages to be used in the arbitral proceedings. Failing such agreement, the arbitral tribunal shall determine the language or languages to be used in the proceedings. This agreement or determination, unless otherwise specified therein, shall apply to any written statement by a party, any hearing and any award, decision or other communication by the arbitral tribunal.

(2) The arbitral tribunal may order that any documentary evidence shall be accompanied by a translation into the language or languages agreed upon by the parties or determined by the arbitral tribunal.

Article 23: Statements of claim and defence

(1) Within the period of time agreed by the parties or determined by the arbitral tribunal, the claimant shall state the facts supporting his claim, the points at issue and the relief or remedy sought, and the respondent shall state his defence in respect of these particulars, unless the parties have otherwise agreed as to the required elements of such statements. The parties may submit with their statements all documents they consider to be relevant or may add a reference to the documents or other evidence they will submit.

(2) Unless otherwise agreed by the parties, either party may amend or supplement his claim or defence during the course of the arbitral proceedings, unless the arbitral tribunal considers it inappropriate to allow such amendment having regard to the delay in making it.

Article 24: Hearings and written proceedings

(1) Subject to any contrary agreement by the parties, the arbitral tribunal shall decide whether to hold oral hearings for the presentation of evidence or for oral argument, or whether the proceedings shall be conducted on the basis of documents and other materials. However, unless the parties have agreed that no hearings shall be held, the arbitral tribunal shall hold such hearings at an appropriate stage of the proceedings, if so requested by a party.

(2) The parties shall be given sufficient advance notice of any hearing and of any meeting of the arbitral tribunal for the purposes of inspection of goods, other property or documents.

(3) All statements, documents or other information supplied to the arbitral tribunal by one party shall be communicated to the other party. Also any expert report or evidentiary document on which the arbitral tribunal may rely in making its decision shall be communicated to the parties.

Article 25: Default of a party

Unless otherwise agreed by the parties, if, without showing sufficient cause,

(a) the claimant fails to communicate his statement of claim in accordance with article 23(1), the arbitral tribunal shall terminate the proceedings;

(b) the respondent fails to communicate his statement of defence in accordance with article 23(1), the arbitral tribunal shall continue the proceedings without treating such failure in itself as an admission of the claimant's allegations;

(c) any party fails to appear at a hearing or to produce documentary evidence, the arbitral tribunal may continue the proceedings and make the award on the evidence before it.

Article 26: Expert appointed by arbitral tribunal

(1) Unless otherwise agreed by the parties, the arbitral tribunal

(a) may appoint one or more experts to report to it on specific issues to be determined by the arbitral tribunal;

(b) may require a party to give the expert any relevant information or to produce, or to provide access to, any relevant documents, goods or other property for his inspection.

(2) Unless otherwise agreed by the parties, if a party so requests or if the arbitral tribunal considers it necessary, the expert shall, after delivery of his written or oral report, participate in a hearing where the parties have the opportunity to put questions to him and to present expert witnesses in order to testify on the points at issue.

Article 27: Court assistance in taking evidence

The arbitral tribunal or a party with the approval of the arbitral tribunal may request from a competent court of this State assistance in taking evidence. The court may execute the request within its competence and according to its rules on taking evidence.

CHAPTER VI. MAKING OF AWARD AND TERMINATION OF PROCEEDINGS

Article 28: Rules applicable to substance of dispute

(1) The arbitral tribunal shall decide the dispute in accordance with such rules of law as are chosen by the parties as applicable to the substance of the dispute. Any designation of the law or legal system of a given State shall be construed, unless otherwise expressed, as directly referring to the substantive law of that State and not to its conflict of laws rules.

(2) Failing any designation by the parties, the arbitral tribunal shall apply the law determined by the conflict of laws rules which it considers applicable.

(3) The arbitral tribunal shall decide *ex aequo et bono* or as *amiable compositeur* only if the parties have expressly authorized it to do so.

(4) In all cases, the arbitral tribunal shall decide in accordance with the terms of the contract and shall take into account the usages of the trade applicable to the transaction.

Article 29: Decision-making by panel of arbitrators

In arbitral proceedings with more than one arbitrator, any decision of the arbitral tribunal shall be made, unless otherwise agreed by the parties, by a majority of all its members. However, questions of procedure may be decided by a presiding arbitrator, if so authorized by the parties or all members of the arbitral tribunal.

Article 30: Settlement

(1) If, during arbitral proceedings, the parties settle the dispute, the arbitral tribunal shall terminate the proceedings and, if requested by the parties and not objected to by the arbitral tribunal, record the settlement in the form of an arbitral award on agreed terms.

(2) An award on agreed terms shall be made in accordance with the provisions of article 31 and shall state that it is an award. Such an award has the same status and effect as any other award on the merits of the case.

Article 31: Form and contents of award

(1) The award shall be made in writing and shall be signed by the arbitrator or arbitrators. In arbitral proceedings with more than one arbitrator, the signatures of the majority of all members of the arbitral tribunal shall suffice, provided that the reason for any omitted signature is stated.

(2) The award shall state the reasons upon which it is based, unless the parties have agreed that no reasons are to be given or the award is an award on agreed terms under article 30.

(3) The award shall state its date and the place of arbitration as deter-

mined in accordance with article 20(1). The award shall be deemed to have been made at that place.

(4) After the award is made, a copy signed by the arbitrators in accordance with paragraph (1) of this article shall be delivered to each party.

Article 32: Termination of proceedings

(1) The arbitral proceedings are terminated by the final award or by an order of the arbitral tribunal in accordance with paragraph (2) of this article.

(2) The arbitral tribunal shall issue an order for the termination of the arbitral proceedings when:

(a) the claimant withdraws his claim, unless the respondent objects thereto and the arbitral tribunal recognizes a legitimate interest on his part in obtaining a final settlement of the dispute;

(b) the parties agree on the termination of the proceedings;

(c) the arbitral tribunal finds that the continuation of the proceedings has for any other reason become unnecessary or impossible.

(3) The mandate of the arbitral tribunal terminates with the termination of the arbitral proceedings, subject to the provisions of articles 33 and 34(4).

Article 33: Correction and interpretation of award; additional award

(1) Within thirty days of receipt of the award, unless another period of time has been agreed upon by the parties:

(a) a party, with notice to the other party, may request the arbitral tribunal to correct in the award any errors in computation, any clerical or typographical errors or any errors of similar nature;

(b) if so agreed by the parties, a party, with notice to the other party, may request the arbitral tribunal to give an interpretation of a specific point or part of the award.

If the arbitral tribunal considers the request to be justified, it shall make the correction or give the interpretation within thirty days of receipt of the request. The interpretation shall form part of the award.

(2) The arbitral tribunal may correct any error of the type referred to in paragraph (1)(a) of this article on its own initiative within thirty days of the date of the award.

(3) Unless otherwise agreed by the parties, a party, with notice to the other party, may request, within thirty days of receipt of the award, the arbitral tribunal to make an additional award as to claims presented in the arbitral proceedings but omitted from the award. If the arbitral tribunal considers the request to be justified, it shall make the additional award within sixty days.

(4) The arbitral tribunal may extend, if necessary, the period of time within which it shall make a correction, interpretation or an additional award under paragraph (1) or (3) of this article.

(5) The provisions of article 31 shall apply to a correction or interpretation of the award or to an additional award.

CHAPTER VII. RECOURSE AGAINST AWARD

Article 34: Application for setting aside as exclusive recourse against arbitral award

(1) Recourse to a court against an arbitral award may be made only by an application for setting aside in accordance with paragraphs (2) and (3) of this article.

(2) An arbitral award may be set aside by the court specified in article 6 only if:

(a) the party making the application furnishes proof that:
  (i) a party to the arbitration agreement referred to in article 7 was under some incapacity; or the said agreement is not valid under the law to which the parties have subjected it or, failing any indication thereon, under the law of this State; or
  (ii) the party making the application was not given proper notice of the appointment of an arbitrator or of the arbitral proceedings or was otherwise unable to present his case; or
  (iii) the award deals with a dispute not contemplated by or not falling within the terms of the submission to arbitration, or contains decisions on matters beyond the scope of the submission to arbitration, provided that, if the decisions on matters submitted to arbitration can be separated from those not so submitted, only that part of the award which contains decisions on matters not submitted to arbitration may be set aside; or
  (iv) the composition of the arbitral tribunal or the arbitral procedure was not in accordance with the agreement of the parties, unless such agreement was in conflict with a provision of this Law from which the parties cannot derogate, or, failing such agreement, was not in accordance with this Law; or
(b) the court finds that:
  (i) the subject-matter of the dispute is not capable of settlement by arbitration under the law of this State; or
  (ii) the award is in conflict with the public policy of this State.

(3) An application for setting aside may not be made after three months have elapsed from the date on which the party making that application had received the award or, if a request had been made under article 33, from the date on which that request had been disposed of by the arbitral tribunal.

(4) The court, when asked to set aside an award, may, where appropriate and so requested by a party, suspend the setting aside proceedings for a period of time determined by it in order to give the arbitral tribunal an opportunity to resume the arbitral proceedings or to take such other action as in the arbitral tribunal's opinion will eliminate the grounds for setting aside.

CHAPTER VIII. RECOGNITION AND ENFORCEMENT OF AWARDS

Article 35: Recognition and enforcement

(1) An arbitral award, irrespective of the country in which it was made, shall be recognized as binding and, upon application in writing to the competent court, shall be enforced subject to the provisions of this article and of article 36.

(2) The party relying on an award or applying for its enforcement shall supply the duly authenticated original award or a duly certified copy thereof, and the original arbitration agreement referred to in article 7 or a duly certified copy thereof. If the award or agreement is not made in an official language of this State, the party shall supply a duly certified translation thereof into such language.[3]

Article 36: Grounds for refusing recognition or enforcement

(1) Recognition or enforcement of an arbitral award, irrespective of the country in which it was made, may be refused only:

(a) at the request of the party against whom it is invoked, if that party furnishes to the competent court where recognition or enforcement is sought proof that:

 (i) a party to the arbitration agreement referred to in article 7 was under some incapacity; or the said agreement is not valid under the law to which the parties have subjected it or, failing any indication thereon, under the law of the country where the award was made; or

 (ii) the party against whom the award is invoked was not given proper notice of the appointment of an arbitrator or of the arbitral proceedings or was otherwise unable to present his case; or

 (iii) the award deals with a dispute not contemplated by or not falling within the terms of the submission to arbitration, or it contains decisions on matters beyond the scope of the submission to arbitration, provided that, if the decisions on matters submitted to arbitration can be separated from those not so submitted, that part of the award which contains decisions on matters submitted to arbitration may be recognized and enforced; or

 (iv) the composition of the arbitral tribunal or the arbitral procedure was not in accordance with the agreement of the parties or, failing such agreement, was not in accordance with the law of the country where the arbitration took place; or

 (v) the award has not yet become binding on the parties or has been set aside or suspended by a court of the country in which, or under the law of which, that award was made; or

(b) if the court finds that:

---

[3] The conditions set forth in this paragraph are intended to set maximum standards. It would, thus, not be contrary to the harmonization to be achieved by the model law if a State retained even less onerous conditions.

(i) the subject-matter of the dispute is not capable of settlement by arbitration under the law of this State; or

(ii) the recognition or enforcement of the award would be contrary to the public policy of this State.

(2) If an application for setting aside or suspension of an award has been made to a court referred to in paragraph (1)(a)(v) of this article, the court where recognition or enforcement is sought may, if it considers it proper, adjourn its decision and may also, on the application of the party claiming recognition or enforcement of the award, order the other party to provide appropriate security.

7 · 'Documents-only' arbitrations

Background to the procedure

In Chapter 1, reference is made to the millions of commercial transactions in which the general public in the United Kingdom are daily engaged, and to the importance in the public interest of finding a means, apart from litigation, by which disputes arising in the course of those transactions may be resolved speedily, economically, privately and, above all, impartially and independently. It is suggested that arbitration constitutes the natural and obvious means; but in practice it may not always be so, if the arbitral procedure employed follows slavishly the procedure in litigation, and imports some of the less attractive features of our adversarial system – as discussed in Chapter 3 – with the possible loss of speed and economy. As we have seen, the main impediments to those desirable objectives derive from (i) the bitterly fought interlocutory applications in which it so often appears that the object is to delay, harass and destroy an opponent's case rather than to elicit the truth, and (ii) the oral presentation at the hearing of argument and evidence. The difficulty, for the arbitrator, in making arrangements for such an oral presentation that suits the convenience (and other commitments) of counsel, solicitors, and expert and other witnesses – particularly where one or other of the parties has formed a gloomy view of the prospects of success of his case – may result in delays of months and years as well as rapidly escalating costs.

There have, of course, always been cases in which the informality of the arbitral procedure involved avoided these problems, and in the United Kingdom the rise of consumerism gave great impetus for such an informal procedure to be devised and employed, at least in relation to the smaller claims. Indeed, in the Arbitration Rules of the Chartered Institute of Arbitrators (1981 edition), reference was made to such a procedure in Article 13 ('Simplified Procedure') as follows:

'Where the value of all matters in dispute between the parties does not exceed £5,000 or *in any other arbitration where the parties so agree*
(1) the Registrar will appoint a single arbitrator.

(2) the arbitrator may determine the dispute at an informal hearing attended by all the parties.
(3) *alternatively, the arbitrator may determine the disputes on the documents submitted to him by the parties, voluntarily or on his direction without any hearing'* (author's italics).

It is noteworthy that the 1988 edition of the Institute's rules (reproduced in Part Two on pages 93–99) does not contain a similar provision. But Article 5 does state:

'5.1 In the absence of procedural rules agreed by the parties or contained herein, the Arbitrator shall have the widest discretion allowed by law to ensure the just, expeditious, economical, and final determination of the dispute.
5.2 Any party wishing the Arbitrator to adopt a simplified or expedited procedure should apply to the Arbitrator for this within 15 days of notification of the Arbitrator's acceptance of his appointment.'

Thus the adoption of 'documents-only' procedure is certainly possible under the 1988 rules; indeed, the matter is carried further by Article 8.1 of these rules, which provides that 'Subject to Article 12, each party has the right to be heard before the Arbitrator unless the parties have agreed to documents-only arbitration.'

So there have existed for many years facilities for arbitrations to be conducted on the basis of submission of documentary argument and evidence.

This does not mean, of course, the exclusion of the professional adviser. On the contrary, there is everything to be said for the preparation of the documentary argument and evidence being undertaken by the professional adviser, particularly where the matter in dispute raises questions of law as well as of fact. For the documents-only arbitration is as much a binding and enforceable decision-making process as a judgment of the High Court. Accordingly, support for this type of arbitration is certainly not based upon a desire to exclude the professional adviser, although some criticism of the procedure has been based upon that premiss. That criticism suggested that parties might 'jump at the chance of getting an arbitration on documents alone' because 'they will not have a lawyer's knowledge of the importance of seeing and questioning a witness'.

Experience of hundreds of cases dealt with on 'documents only' has tended to show that in fact the careful study of properly prepared written submissions and all relevant documents, coupled with a site visit where appropriate, leads to a conclusion more reliable than one based upon oral evidence, given perhaps years after the event in an aggressive and hostile environment.

National Small Claims Arbitration Service

The positive experience of documents-only procedure supplied the impetus for the setting-up in 1975 by the Chartered Institute of Arbitrators of a National Small Claims Arbitration Service. This service provides for the settlement of disputes and differences between subscribers to the service and their customers where the normal dispute procedure has failed to achieve an amicable settlement.

The service offers a simple and inexpensive method of resolving disputes by the appointment of an independent arbitrator to give a ruling quickly and with the minimum of formality. In normal circumstances proceedings can be completed within three months of the date of the Institute's acceptance of an application. The rules commit the parties to a very modest financial outlay in respect of the administration of the arbitration which may be recovered by the successful party.

The entitlement of parties to take advantage of the service is as specified in the relevant contractual documents, and the relevant Code of Practice, if any. Applications have to be made on the prescribed form and the parties have to agree to be bound by the arbitrator's decision.

Informality is the essence of the service. The arbitrator appointed by the President, or a Vice-President, of the Institute decides disputes by reference to written submissions and documentary evidence supplied by the parties, with no oral hearing.

The arbitrators selected for appointment are from the Institute's Arbitrator Panel membership and all appointments are within the Institute's exclusive and unfettered control.

The rules of the Small Claims Service are not designed to accommodate disputes in which, in the opinion of the arbitrator, there are unusually complicated issues, the proper resolution of which is likely to require a hearing and oral evidence.

The setting-up of the Small Claims Service happened at about the same time as the Office of Fair Trading was established and began to promote the principle of self-regulation in commercial and financial services and transactions. Trade associations and other organisations which provided such services to the consumer, either directly or through constituent members, were encouraged by the Office of Fair Trading to provide Codes of Practice on fair dealing, by which provision was made for investigation and conciliation in respect of complaints and disputes. But these Codes of practice clearly could not stop there, since, if a member of an association failed to honour his obligations under the code, what redress, other than litigation, had the consumer claimant? This is where the Chartered Institute of Arbitrators' service, as a completely independent and impartial element, filled the gap.

Since the introduction of the Small Claims Service, Codes of Practice have been formed for many trade and service organisations, containing provision for reference to arbitration of consumer disputes that cannot be resolved by negotiation. Special schemes have been devised for the travel industry (ABTA and others), the holiday caravan industry, the oil industry, electricity services and supplies, the Post Office, British Telecom and related services, British Rail, the Law Society, personal insurance (to which more than 50 companies adhere) and many other industries and services. These schemes vary in detail, but all are based on the principles and rules of the Small Claims Service described above.

A registration fee is payable by each party when an application for arbitration under the Small Claims Service is submitted, on a scale set out in the application form. They are applied towards defraying the Institute's administrative costs and are non-returnable except as mentioned below, although either party may be required to reimburse the other's registration fee.

Documents-only procedure

Subject to any directions issued by the arbitrator and to the provisions of Rules 1(a) and 2(e) below, the arbitration will be on *documents only* and the procedure is as follows:

1. General

(a) The party making the claim (the 'claimant') is required, within 28 days of receipt of the claim form, to send the completed form, together with the supporting documents in duplicate, to the Institute. (The customer may not, without the consent of the Institute, claim an amount greater than specified on the application for arbitration.)

(b) A copy of the claim documents will be sent by the Institute to the other party (the 'respondent'), who is required, within 28 days of receipt of the documents, to send to the Institute his written defence to the claim together with any supporting documents in duplicate. (The respondent may include with his defence a counterclaim in respect of any balance of payment alleged to be due on the contract between the parties. The respondent may not, without the consent of the Institute, make any other counterclaim against the claimant unless such counterclaim is admissible under the Service as applicable to disputes between the parties and notice thereof was contained in the parties' application for arbitration.)

(c) A copy of the defence documents will be sent by the Institute to the claimant, who is entitled to send to the Institute any written comments which he wishes to make on the defence documents within 14 days of their receipt. Such comments should be in duplicate, and may not introduce any new matters or points of claim.

(d) The President, or a Vice-President, of the Institute, at such stage of the proceedings as the Institute considers appropriate, will appoint a sole arbitrator to decide the dispute and the Institute will notify the parties of his appointment.

(e) The arbitrator will make his award with reference to the documents submitted by the parties and transmit his award to the Institute for publication.

(f) Unless the parties otherwise agree, the arbitrator's reasons will be set out or referred to in his award.

(g) The Institute will publish the award by sending copies to each of the parties. In normal circumstances the Institute will also send a copy to the trade association concerned.

(h) Unless directed otherwise in the award, within 21 days of despatch to the parties of the copy award, payment shall be made of any monies directed by the award to be paid. Such payment shall be made by the party liable direct to the party entitled, and not through the Institute.

2. Supplementary

(a) The arbitrator may, through the Registrar [of the Institute], request the provision of any further documents/information which he considers would assist him in his decision. If the documents/information are not supplied to the Institute within such time as it prescribes, the arbitrator will proceed with the reference on the basis of the documents already before him.

(b) Where in the opinion of the arbitrator it is desirable, he may make an examination of the subject matter of the dispute. The parties shall afford the arbitrator all necessary assistance and facilities for the conduct of this examination.

(c) Where appropriate, the arbitrator may sit with one or more independent technical advisers appointed by the Institute when considering the documentary evidence submitted to him.

(d) Where, in the opinion of the arbitrator, it is desirable that independent examination of the subject matter of the dispute be made, an independent examiner will be appointed by the Institute to make such examination and a written report thereon. The parties shall afford the examiner all necessary assistance and facilities for the conduct of this examination and copies of his report shall be sent by the Institute to the parties, who will then be given 14 days in which to comment thereon.

(e) If the claimant does not furnish his claim within the time allowed and does not remedy his default within 14 days after despatch to him by the Institute of notice of that default, he will be treated as having abandoned his claim. The arbitration will not proceed and the respondent's registration fee will be returned to him.

(f) If the respondent does not furnish his defence within the time allowed and does not remedy his default within 14 days after despatch to him by the Institute of notice of that default, the arbitrator will be appointed and subject to any directions he may give the dispute will be decided by him by reference to the documents submitted by the claimant.

(g) If, in the opinion of the arbitrator, the dispute is not capable of proper resolution on documents only, he shall advise the parties through the Institute with his proposals for how else the arbitration should proceed. If the parties accept these proposals the arbitration shall proceed accordingly, provided that the special costs provisions of the Rules shall no longer apply. Failing such agreement the arbitrator's appointment shall be deemed revoked and the parties' application for arbitration deemed withdrawn, and the parties' registration fees will be refunded. The claimant will then be at liberty to pursue the matter through the courts.

Costs

3. The arbitrator's fees and expenses shall be paid by the Institute and are part of the administrative costs of the Service.

4. The administrative costs of the Service, of any independent technical adviser under Rule 2(c), and of any independent examiner under Rule 2(d), are subject to a separate agreement between the Institute and subscribers to the National Small Claims Arbitration Service.

5. Each party bears its own costs of preparing and submitting its case.

6. The arbitrator has a discretion to give in his award such directions as he considers appropriate with regard to reimbursement

of either party by the other of the amount of its registration fee.

Enforcement

7. (a) The law to apply (English, Scottish, etc.) may be determined by the arbitrator if the parties fail to agree.

(b) Where Scottish law applies, any reference in these Rules to an arbitrator shall be construed as a reference to an arbiter.

8. The Institute reserves the right to appoint a substitute arbitrator if the arbitrator originally appointed dies or is incapacitated or is for any reason unable to deal expeditiously with the dispute. The parties shall be notified of any substitution.

9. Awards made under the Services are final and binding on the parties. Subject to the right of a party to request the Institute to draw the arbitrator's attention to any accidental slip or omission which he has power to correct, neither the Institute nor the arbitrator can enter into correspondence regarding awards made under the Service.

Appeals

10. Rights of application or appeal (if any) to the courts are as under the relevant Arbitration Acts provided that:

(a) The special costs provisions of the Service shall not apply to any such application or appeal;

(b) Either party making any such application or appeal (other than an application for leave to enforce the award) will bear its own and the other parties' costs (including the costs of any resumed or fresh arbitration resulting from such proceedings) irrespective of the outcome of such proceedings.

11. Neither the Institute nor the arbitrator shall be liable to any party for any act or omission in connection with any arbitration conducted under these Rules save that the arbitrator (but not the Institute) shall be liable for any conscious or deliberate wrongdoing on his own part.

Consumer arbitration – a summary

As noted earlier, in some of the individual administered schemes there are departures from the detailed structure and procedure outlined above; for example, in the scheme operating for the Personal Insurance Arbitration Service, the costs of the arbitration are wholly borne by the insurance company in any event. But the main features of a 'consumer' arbitration are preserved in all cases, and may be summarised as follows:

1. It is a real arbitration, conducted under the relative statutory provisions discussed in Chapter 3 and set out in Part Two (pages 61–92). It results in an enforceable award, in the same way as a judgment of the High Court.
2. It normally arises at the instance of the claimant consumer, the respondent being required by the relative Code of Practice or prior agreement to acquiesce in the application.
3. The liability of the claimant to bear the costs of the arbitration is strictly limited and known in advance. It is confined to payment of a registration fee, normally a nominal sum not exceeding £15, which may be refunded to the claimant. However, in a case where there is no merit in the claim, the unsuccessful claimant may be ordered to pay the respondent's registration fee as well as his own. The remaining costs of the arbitration are borne by the trade association or other organisation 'sponsoring' the scheme.
4. Each of the individual parties bears his costs of preparing and submitting his case. This feature, like that mentioned in paragraph 3 above, is authorised by s. 18(3) of the Arbitration Act 1950, since the agreement to arbitrate is made after the dispute has arisen.
5. Finally, all schemes contemplate that conclusions will be reached on documents only, i.e. the submission of considered written statements and documentary evidence to support them.

There is no doubt that these administered schemes of consumer arbitration have been most successful in achieving the objectives set for them – the resolution of consumer disputes speedily, efficiently, inexpensively and, above all, impartially and enforceably. Having operated these schemes since 1975, the Institute is now processing a thousand cases a year, and the throughput seems likely to grow.

One of the most important aspects of these administered schemes is that they have provided, as it were, extensive 'field trials' of documents-only arbitration; and have demonstrated the benefits of the system both to the business world and to the general public. It is to be hoped that this experience will be used in an ever-widening area in the world of commercial arbitration. The documents-only system, coupled where appropriate with a site visit, has already proved itself in a variety of fields, including agricultural disputes (e.g. allocation of milk quota on division of a dairy produce holding) and medical partnership disputes. It can serve many more.

Part Two · *Statutes and rules*

Arbitration Act 1950

ARRANGEMENT OF SECTIONS

PART I

GENERAL PROVISIONS AS TO ARBITRATION

Effect of Arbitration Agreements, &c.

CHAPTER 27

An Act to consolidate the Arbitration Acts, 1889 to 1934.
[28th July 1950.]

BE it enacted by the King's most Excellent Majesty, by and with the advice and consent of the Lords Spiritual and Temporal, and Commons, in this present Parliament assembled, and by the authority of the same, as follows:—

PART I

GENERAL PROVISIONS AS TO ARBITRATION

Effect of Arbitration Agreements, &c.

1. The authority of an arbitrator or umpire appointed by or by virtue of an arbitration agreement shall, unless a contrary intention is expressed in the agreement, be irrevocable except by leave of the High Court or a judge thereof. *[margin: Authority of arbitrators and umpires to be irrevocable.]*

2.—(1) An arbitration agreement shall not be discharged by the death of any party thereto, either as respects the deceased or any other party, but shall in such an event be enforceable by or against the personal representative of the deceased. *[margin: Death of party.]*

(2) The authority of an arbitrator shall not be revoked by the death of any party by whom he was appointed.

(3) Nothing in this section shall be taken to affect the operation of any enactment or rule of law by virtue of which any right of action is extinguished by the death of a person.

3.—(1) Where it is provided by a term in a contract to which a bankrupt is a party that any differences arising thereout or in connection therewith shall be referred to arbitration, the said term shall, if the trustee in bankruptcy adopts the contract, be enforceable by or against him so far as relates to any such differences. *[margin: Bankruptcy.]*

PART I
—cont.

(2) Where a person who has been adjudged bankrupt had, before the commencement of the bankruptcy, become a party to an arbitration agreement, and any matter to which the agreement applies requires to be determined in connection with or for the purposes of the bankruptcy proceedings, then, if the case is one to which subsection (1) of this section does not apply, any other party to the agreement or, with the consent of the committee of inspection, the trustee in bankruptcy, may apply to the court having jurisdiction in the bankruptcy proceedings for an order directing that the matter in question shall be referred to arbitration in accordance with the agreement, and that court may, if it is of opinion that, having regard to all the circumstances of the case, the matter ought to be determined by arbitration, make an order accordingly.

Staying court proceedings where there is submission to arbitration.

4.—(1) If any party to an arbitration agreement, or any person claiming through or under him, commences any legal proceedings in any court against any other party to the agreement, or any person claiming through or under him, in respect of any matter agreed to be referred, any party to those legal proceedings may at any time after appearance, and before delivering any pleadings or taking any other steps in the proceedings, apply to that court to stay the proceedings, and that court or a judge thereof, if satisfied that there is no sufficient reason why the matter should not be referred in accordance with the agreement, and that the applicant was, at the time when the proceedings were commenced, and still remains, ready and willing to do all things necessary to the proper conduct of the arbitration, may make an order staying the proceedings.

(2)* Notwithstanding anything in this Part of this Act, if any party to a submission to arbitration made in pursuance of an agreement to which the protocol set out in the First Schedule to this Act applies, or any person claiming through or under him, commences any legal proceedings in any court against any other party to the submission, or any person claiming through or under him, in respect of any matter agreed to be referred, any party to those legal proceedings may at any time after appearance, and before delivering any pleadings or taking any other steps in the proceedings, apply to that court to stay the proceedings, and that court or a judge thereof, unless satisfied that the agreement or arbitration has become inoperative or cannot proceed or that there is not in fact any dispute between the parties with regard to the matter agreed to be referred, shall make an order staying the proceedings.

Reference of interpleader issues to arbitration.

5. Where relief by way of interpleader is granted and it appears to the High Court that the claims in question are matters to which an arbitration agreement, to which the claimants are parties, applies, the High Court may direct the issue between the claimants to be determined in accordance with the agreement.

* Section 4(2) repealed by s. 8(2)(d), Arbitration Act 1975.

Arbitrators and Umpires

6. Unless a contrary intention is expressed therein, every When reference arbitration agreement shall, if no other mode of reference is is to a single provided, be deemed to include a provision that the reference arbitrator. shall be to a single arbitrator.

7. Where an arbitration agreement provides that the reference Power of shall be to two arbitrators, one to be appointed by each party, parties in then, unless a contrary intention is expressed therein— certain cases to supply

    (*a*) if either of the appointed arbitrators refuses to act, or vacancy. is incapable of acting, or dies, the party who appointed him may appoint a new arbitrator in his place ;

    (*b*) if, on such a reference, one party fails to appoint an arbitrator, either originally, or by way of substitution as aforesaid, for seven clear days after the other party, having appointed his arbitrator, has served the party making default with notice to make the appointment, the party who has appointed an arbitrator may appoint that arbitrator to act as sole arbitrator in the reference and his award shall be binding on both parties as if he had been appointed by consent:

Provided that the High Court or a judge thereof may set aside any appointment made in pursuance of this section.

8.—(1)* Unless a contrary intention is expressed therein, every Umpires. arbitration agreement shall, where the reference is to two arbitrators, be deemed to include a provision that the two arbitrators shall appoint an umpire immediately after they are themselves appointed.

(2) Unless a contrary intention is expressed therein, every arbitration agreement shall, where such a provision is applicable to the reference, be deemed to include a provision that if the arbitrators have delivered to any party to the arbitration agreement, or to the umpire, a notice in writing stating that they cannot agree, the umpire may forthwith enter on the reference in lieu of the arbitrators.

(3) At any time after the appointment of an umpire, however appointed, the High Court may, on the application of any party to the reference and notwithstanding anything to the contrary in the arbitration agreement, order that the umpire shall enter upon the reference in lieu of the arbitrators and as if he were a sole arbitrator.

9.—(1)† Where an arbitration agreement provides that the Agreements reference shall be to three arbitrators, one to be appointed by for reference each party and the third to be appointed by the two appointed to three by the parties, the agreement shall have effect as if it provided arbitrators. for the appointment of an umpire, and not for the appointment

* Section 8(1) amended by s. 6(1) Arbitration Act 1979.
† Section 9 amended by s. 6(2) Arbitration Act 1979.

of a third arbitrator, by the two arbitrators appointed by the parties.

(2) Where an arbitration agreement provides that the reference shall be to three arbitrators to be appointed otherwise than as mentioned in subsection (1) of this section, the award of any two of the arbitrators shall be binding.

Power of court in certain cases to appoint an arbitrator or umpire.

10.* In any of the following cases—

(*a*) where an arbitration agreement provides that the reference shall be to a single arbitrator, and all the parties do not, after differences have arisen, concur in the appointment of an arbitrator ;

(*b*) if an appointed arbitrator refuses to act, or is incapable of acting, or dies, and the arbitration agreement does not show that it was intended that the vacancy should not be supplied and the parties do not supply the vacancy ;

(*c*) where the parties or two arbitrators are at liberty to appoint an umpire or third arbitrator and do not appoint him, or where two arbitrators are required to appoint an umpire and do not appoint him ;

(*d*) where an appointed umpire or third arbitrator refuses to act, or is incapable of acting, or dies, and the arbitration agreement does not show that it was intended that the vacancy should not be supplied, and the parties or arbitrators do not supply the vacancy ;

any party may serve the other parties or the arbitrators, as the case may be, with a written notice to appoint or, as the case may be, concur in appointing, an arbitrator, umpire or third arbitrator, and if the appointment is not made within seven clear days after the service of the notice, the High Court or a judge thereof may, on application by the party who gave the notice, appoint an arbitrator, umpire or third arbitrator who shall have the like powers to act in the reference and make an award as if he had been appointed by consent of all parties.

Reference to official referee.

11. Where an arbitration agreement provides that the reference shall be to an official referee, any official referee to whom application is made shall, subject to any order of the High Court or a judge thereof as to transfer or otherwise, hear and determine the matters agreed to be referred.

Conduct of Proceedings, Witnesses, &c.

Conduct of proceedings, witnesses, &c.

12.—(1) Unless a contrary intention is expressed therein, every arbitration agreement shall, where such a provision is applicable to the reference, be deemed to contain a provision that the parties to the reference, and all persons claiming through them respectively, shall, subject to any legal objection, submit to

* Section 10 amended by ss. 6(3) and 6(4) Arbitration Act 1979.

be examined by the arbitrator or umpire, on oath or affirmation, in relation to the matters in dispute, and shall, subject as aforesaid, produce before the arbitrator or umpire all documents within their possession or power respectively which may be required or called for, and do all other things which during the proceedings on the reference the arbitrator or umpire may require.

(2) Unless a contrary intention is expressed therein, every arbitration agreement shall, where such a provision is applicable to the reference, be deemed to contain a provision that the witnesses on the reference shall, if the arbitrator or umpire thinks fit, be examined on oath or affirmation.

(3) An arbitrator or umpire shall, unless a contrary intention is expressed in the arbitration agreement, have power to administer oaths to, or take the affirmations of, the parties to and witnesses on a reference under the agreement.

(4) Any party to a reference under an arbitration agreement may sue out a writ of subpoena ad testificandum or a writ of subpoena duces tecum, but no person shall be compelled under any such writ to produce any document which he could not be compelled to produce on the trial of an action, and the High Court or a judge thereof may order that a writ of subpoena ad testificandum or of subpoena duces tecum shall issue to compel the attendance before an arbitrator or umpire of a witness wherever he may be within the United Kingdom.

(5) The High Court or a judge thereof may also order that a writ of habeas corpus ad testificandum shall issue to bring up a prisoner for examination before an arbitrator or umpire.

(6) The High Court shall have, for the purpose of and in relation to a reference, the same power of making orders in respect of—

(a) security for costs ;

(b) discovery of documents and interrogatories ;

(c) the giving of evidence by affidavit ;

(d) examination on oath of any witness before an officer of the High Court or any other person, and the issue of a commission or request for the examination of a witness out of the jurisdiction ;

(e) the preservation, interim custody or sale of any goods which are the subject matter of the reference ;

(f) securing the amount in dispute in the reference ;

(g) the detention, preservation or inspection of any property or thing which is the subject of the reference or as to which any question may arise therein, and authorising for any of the purposes aforesaid any persons to enter

PART I
—cont.

upon or into any land or building in the possession of any party to the reference, or authorising any samples to be taken or any observation to be made or experiment to be tried which may be necessary or expedient for the purpose of obtaining full information or evidence ; and

(h) interim injunctions or the appointment of a receiver ;

as it has for the purpose of and in relation to an action or matter in the High Court:

Provided that nothing in this subsection shall be taken to prejudice any power which may be vested in an arbitrator or umpire of making orders with respect to any of the matters aforesaid.*

Provisions as to Awards

Time for
making award.

13.—(1) Subject to the provisions of subsection (2) of section twenty-two of this Act, and anything to the contrary in the arbitration agreement, an arbitrator or umpire shall have power to make an award at any time.

(2) The time, if any, limited for making an award, whether under this Act or otherwise, may from time to time be enlarged by order of the High Court or a judge thereof, whether that time has expired or not.

(3) The High Court may, on the application of any party to a reference, remove an arbitrator or umpire who fails to use all reasonable dispatch in entering on and proceeding with the reference and making an award, and an arbitrator or umpire who is removed by the High Court under this subsection shall not be entitled to receive any remuneration in respect of his services.

For the purposes of this subsection, the expression " proceeding with a reference " includes, in a case where two arbitrators are unable to agree, giving notice of that fact to the parties and to the umpire.

Interim
awards.

14. Unless a contrary intention is expressed therein, every arbitration agreement shall, where such a provision is applicable to the reference, be deemed to contain a provision that the arbitrator or umpire may, if he thinks fit, make an interim award, and any reference in this Part of this Act to an award includes a reference to an interim award.

Specific
performance.

15. Unless a contrary intention is expressed therein, every arbitration agreement shall, where such a provision is applicable to the reference, be deemed to contain a provision that the arbitrator or umpire shall have the same power as the High Court to order specific performance of any contract other than a contract relating to land or any interest in land.

* See also s. 5 Arbitration Act 1979, and the rules of the Chartered Institute of Arbitrators (Article 11) and of the London Court of International Arbitration (Article 13) as to power of arbitrator to make interlocutory orders.

16. Unless a contrary intention is expressed therein, every arbitration agreement shall, where such a provision is applicable to the reference, be deemed to contain a provision that the award to be made by the arbitrator or umpire shall be final and binding on the parties and the persons claiming under them respectively.

PART I
—*cont.*
Awards to be final.

17. Unless a contrary intention is expressed in the arbitration agreement, the arbitrator or umpire shall have power to correct in an award any clerical mistake or error arising from any accidental slip or omission.

Power to correct slips.

Costs, Fees and Interest

18.—(1) Unless a contrary intention is expressed therein, every arbitration agreement shall be deemed to include a provision that the costs of the reference and award shall be in the discretion of the arbitrator or umpire, who may direct to and by whom and in what manner those costs or any part thereof shall be paid, and may tax or settle the amount of costs to be so paid or any part thereof, and may award costs to be paid as between solicitor and client.

Costs.

(2) Any costs directed by an award to be paid shall, unless the award otherwise directs, be taxable in the High Court.

(3) Any provision in an arbitration agreement to the effect that the parties or any party thereto shall in any event pay their or his own costs of the reference or award or any part thereof shall be void, and this Part of this Act shall, in the case of an arbitration agreement containing any such provision, have effect as if that provision were not contained therein :

Provided that nothing in this subsection shall invalidate such a provision when it is a part of an agreement to submit to arbitration a dispute which has arisen before the making of that agreement.

(4) If no provision is made by an award with respect to the costs of the reference, any party to the reference may, within fourteen days of the publication of the award or such further time as the High Court or a judge thereof may direct, apply to the arbitrator for an order directing by and to whom those costs shall be paid, and thereupon the arbitrator shall, after hearing any party who may desire to be heard, amend his award by adding thereto such directions as he may think proper with respect to the payment of the costs of the reference.

(5) Section sixty-nine of the Solicitors Act, 1932 (which empowers a court before which any proceeding is being heard or is pending to charge property recovered or preserved in the

PART I
—*cont.*

proceeding with the payment of solicitors' costs) shall apply as if an arbitration were a proceeding in the High Court, and the High Court may make declarations and orders accordingly.

Taxation of arbitrator's or umpire's fees.

19.—(1) If in any case an arbitrator or umpire refuses to deliver his award except on payment of the fees demanded by him, the High Court may, on an application for the purpose, order that the arbitrator or umpire shall deliver the award to the applicant on payment into court by the applicant of the fees demanded, and further that the fees demanded shall be taxed by the taxing officer and that out of the money paid into court there shall be paid out to the arbitrator or umpire by way of fees such sum as may be found reasonable on taxation and that the balance of the money, if any, shall be paid out to the applicant.

(2) An application for the purposes of this section may be made by any party to the reference unless the fees demanded have been fixed by a written agreement between him and the arbitrator or umpire.

(3) A taxation of fees under this section may be reviewed in the same manner as a taxation of costs.

(4) The arbitrator or umpire shall be entitled to appear and be heard on any taxation or review of taxation under this section.

Interest on awards.

20. A sum directed to be paid by an award shall, unless the award otherwise directs, carry interest as from the date of the award and at the same rate as a judgment debt.

Special Cases, Remission and Setting aside of Awards, &c.

Statement of case.

21.—(1)* An arbitrator or umpire may, and shall if so directed by the High Court, state—

   (a) any question of law arising in the course of the reference ; or

   (b) an award or any part of an award,

in the form of a special case for the decision of the High Court.

(2) A special case with respect to an interim award or with respect to a question of law arising in the course of a reference may be stated, or may be directed by the High Court to be stated, notwithstanding that proceedings under the reference are still pending.

(3) A decision of the High Court under this section shall be deemed to be a judgment of the Court within the meaning of section twenty-seven of the Supreme Court of Judicature (Consolidation) Act, 1925 (which relates to the jurisdiction of the Court of Appeal to hear and determine appeals from any judgment of the High Court), but no appeal shall lie from the

* Section 21(1) repealed by s. 8(3)(b) Arbitration Act 1979.

decision of the High Court on any case stated under paragraph (a) of subsection (1) of this section without the leave of the High Court or of the Court of Appeal.

22.—(1) In all cases of reference to arbitration the High Court or a judge thereof may from time to time remit the matters referred, or any of them, to the reconsideration of the arbitrator or umpire.

(2) Where an award is remitted, the arbitrator or umpire shall, unless the order otherwise directs, make his award within three months after the date of the order.

23.—(1) Where an arbitrator or umpire has misconducted himself or the proceedings, the High Court may remove him.

(2) Where an arbitrator or umpire has misconducted himself or the proceedings, or an arbitration or award has been improperly procured, the High Court may set the award aside.

(3) Where an application is made to set aside an award, the High Court may order that any money made payable by the award shall be brought into court or otherwise secured pending the determination of the application.

24.—(1) Where an agreement between any parties provides that disputes which may arise in the future between them shall be referred to an arbitrator named or designated in the agreement, and after a dispute has arisen any party applies, on the ground that the arbitrator so named or designated is not or may not be impartial, for leave to revoke the authority of the arbitrator or for an injunction to restrain any other party or the arbitrator from proceeding with the arbitration, it shall not be a ground for refusing the application that the said party at the time when he made the agreement knew, or ought to have known, that the arbitrator, by reason of his relation towards any other party to the agreement or of his connection with the subject referred, might not be capable of impartiality.

(2) Where an agreement between any parties provides that disputes which may arise in the future between them shall be referred to arbitration, and a dispute which so arises involves the question whether any such party has been guilty of fraud, the High Court shall, so far as may be necessary to enable that question to be determined by the High Court, have power to order that the agreement shall cease to have effect and power to give leave to revoke the authority of any arbitrator or umpire appointed by or by virtue of the agreement.

(3) In any case where by virtue of this section the High Court has power to order that an arbitration agreement shall cease to have effect or to give leave to revoke the authority of an arbitrator or umpire, the High Court may refuse to stay any action brought in breach of the agreement.

PART I
—*cont.*
Power of
court where
arbitrator is
removed or
authority of
arbitrator is
revoked.

25.—(1) Where an arbitrator (not being a sole arbitrator), or two or more arbitrators (not being all the arbitrators) or an umpire who has not entered on the reference is or are removed by the High Court, the High Court may, on the application of any party to the arbitration agreement, appoint a person or persons to act as arbitrator or arbitrators or umpire in place of the person or persons so removed.

(2) Where the authority of an arbitrator or arbitrators or umpire is revoked by leave of the High Court, or a sole arbitrator or all the arbitrators or an umpire who has entered on the reference is or are removed by the High Court, the High Court may, on the application of any party to the arbitration agreement, either—

    (*a*) appoint a person to act as sole arbitrator in place of the person or persons removed ; or

    (*b*) order that the arbitration agreement shall cease to have effect with respect to the dispute referred.

(3) A person appointed under this section by the High Court as an arbitrator or umpire shall have the like power to act in the reference and to make an award as if he had been appointed in accordance with the terms of the arbitration agreement.

(4) Where it is provided (whether by means of a provision in the arbitration agreement or otherwise) that an award under an arbitration agreement shall be a condition precedent to the bringing of an action with respect to any matter to which the agreement applies, the High Court, if it orders (whether under this section or under any other enactment) that the agreement shall cease to have effect as regards any particular dispute, may further order that the provision making an award a condition precedent to the bringing of an action shall also cease to have effect as regards that dispute.

Enforcement of Award

26. An award on an arbitration agreement may, by leave of the High Court or a judge thereof, be enforced in the same manner as a judgment or order to the same effect, and where leave is so given, judgment may be entered in terms of the award.

Miscellaneous

Power of
court to
extend time for
commencing
arbitration
proceedings.

27. Where the terms of an agreement to refer future disputes to arbitration provide that any claims to which the agreement applies shall be barred unless notice to appoint an arbitrator is given or an arbitrator is appointed or some other step to commence arbitration proceedings is taken within a time fixed by the agreement, and a dispute arises to which the agreement applies, the High Court, if it is of opinion that in the circumstances of the case undue hardship would otherwise be caused,

and notwithstanding that the time so fixed has expired, may, PART I
on such terms, if any, as the justice of the case may require, —*cont.*
but without prejudice to the provisions of any enactment limiting the time for the commencement of arbitration proceedings, extend the time for such period as it thinks proper.

28. Any order made under this Part of this Act may be made Terms as to on such terms as to costs or otherwise as the authority making costs, &c. the order thinks just :

Provided that this section shall not apply to any order made under subsection (2) of section four of this Act.*

29.—(1) In subsection (3) of section four hundred and ninety- Extension of six of the Merchant Shipping Act, 1894 (which requires a sum s. 496 of the deposited with a wharfinger by an owner of goods to be repaid Merchant unless legal proceedings are instituted by the shipowner), the Shipping Act, expression "legal proceedings" shall be deemed to include 1894. arbitration.

(2) For the purposes of the said section four hundred and ninety-six, as amended by this section, an arbitration shall be deemed to be commenced when one party to the arbitration agreement serves on the other party or parties a notice requiring him or them to appoint or concur in appointing an arbitrator, or, where the arbitration agreement provides that the reference shall be to a person named or designated in the agreement, requiring him or them to submit the dispute to the person so named or designated.

(3) Any such notice as is mentioned in subsection (2) of this section may be served either—

> (a) by delivering it to the person on whom it is to be served ; or
>
> (b) by leaving it at the usual or last known place of abode in England of that person ; or
>
> (c) by sending it by post in a registered letter addressed to that person at his usual or last known place of abode in England ;

as well as in any other manner provided in the arbitration agreement ; and where a notice is sent by post in manner prescribed by paragraph (c) of this subsection, service thereof shall, unless the contrary is proved, be deemed to have been effected at the time at which the letter would have been delivered in the ordinary course of post.

30. This Part of this Act (except the provisions of subsection Crown to be (2) of section four thereof) shall apply to any arbitration to bound. which His Majesty, either in right of the Crown or of the Duchy of Lancaster or otherwise, or the Duke of Cornwall, is a party. †

* Proviso repealed by s. 8(2)(*b*) Arbitration Act 1975.
† Exception repealed by s. 8(2)(*c*) Arbitration Act 1975.

PART I
—*cont.*
Application of
Part I to
statutory
arbitrations.

31.—(1) Subject to the provisions of section thirty-three of this Act, this Part of this Act, except the provisions thereof specified in subsection (2) of this section, shall apply to every arbitration under any other Act (whether passed before or after the commencement of this Act) as if the arbitration were pursuant to an arbitration agreement and as if that other Act were an arbitration agreement, except in so far as this Act is inconsistent with that other Act or with any rules or procedure authorised or recognised thereby.

(2) The provisions referred to in subsection (1) of this section are subsection (1) of section two, section three, subsection (2) of section four,* section five, subsection (3) of section eighteen and sections twenty-four, twenty-five, twenty-seven and twenty-nine.

Meaning of
" arbitration
agreement".

32. In this Part of this Act, unless the context otherwise requires, the expression " arbitration agreement " means a written agreement to submit present or future differences to arbitration, whether an arbitrator is named therein or not.

Operation of
Part I.

33. This Part of this Act shall not affect any arbitration commenced (within the meaning of subsection (2) of section twenty-nine of this Act) before the commencement of this Act, but shall apply to an arbitration so commenced after the commencement of this Act under an agreement made before the commencement of this Act.

Extent of
Part I.

34. Subsection (2) of section four of this Act shall—

(a) extend to Scotland, with the omission of the words " Notwithstanding anything in this Part of this Act " and with the substitution, for references to staying proceedings, of references to sisting proceedings ; and

(b) extend to Northern Ireland, with the omission of the words " Notwithstanding anything in this Part of this Act " ;

but, save† as aforesaid, none of the provisions of this Part of this Act shall extend to Scotland or Northern Ireland.

PART II
ENFORCEMENT OF CERTAIN FOREIGN AWARDS

Awards to
which Part II
applies.

35.—(1) This Part of this Act applies to any award made after the twenty-eighth day of July, nineteen hundred and twenty-four—

(a) in pursuance of an agreement for arbitration to which the protocol set out in the First Schedule to this Act applies ; and

(b) between persons of whom one is subject to the jurisdiction of some one of such Powers as His Majesty, being satisfied that reciprocal provisions have been

---

* Section 4(2) repealed by s. 8(2)(d) Arbitration Act 1975.

† Section 34(a) and (b) repealed by s. 8(2)(e) Arbitration Act 1975.

made, may by Order in Council declare to be parties to **PART II**
the convention set out in the Second Schedule to this *—cont.*
Act, and of whom the other is subject to the jurisdiction of some other of the Powers aforesaid ; and

(c) in one of such territories as His Majesty, being satisfied
that reciprocal provisions have been made, may by
Order in Council declare to be territories to which the
the said convention applies ;

and an award to which this Part of this Act applies is in this
Part of this Act referred to as " a foreign award ".

(2) His Majesty may by a subsequent Order in Council vary
or revoke any Order previously made under this section.

(3) Any Order in Council under section one of the Arbitration
(Foreign Awards) Act, 1930, which is in force at the commencement of this Act shall have effect as if it had been made under
this section.

36.—(1) A foreign award shall, subject to the provisions of Effect of
this Part of this Act, be enforceable in England either by action foreign awards.
or in the same manner as the award of an arbitrator is enforceable by virtue of section twenty-six of this Act.

(2) Any foreign award which would be enforceable under this
Part of this Act shall be treated as binding for all purposes on
the persons as between whom it was made, and may accordingly
be relied on by any of those persons by way of defence, set off or
otherwise in any legal proceedings in England, and any references
in this Part of this Act to enforcing a foreign award shall be
construed as including references to relying on an award.

37.—(1) In order that a foreign award may be enforceable Conditions for
under this Part of this Act it must have— enforcement
of foreign
(a) been made in pursuance of an agreement for arbitration awards.
which was valid under the law by which it was
governed ;

(b) been made by the tribunal provided for in the agreement
or constituted in manner agreed upon by the parties ;

(c) been made in conformity with the law governing the
arbitration procedure ;

(d) become final in the country in which it was made ;

(e) been in respect of a matter which may lawfully be
referred to arbitration under the law of England ;

and the enforcement thereof must not be contrary to the public
policy or the law of England.

(2) Subject to the provisions of this subsection, a foreign award
shall not be enforceable under this Part of this Act if the court
dealing with the case is satisfied that—

(a) the award has been annulled in the country in which it
was made ; or

(b) the party against whom it is sought to enforce the award was not given notice of the arbitration proceedings in sufficient time to enable him to present his case, or was under some legal incapacity and was not properly represented ; or

(c) the award does not deal with all the questions referred or contains decisions on matters beyond the scope of the agreement for arbitration :

Provided that, if the award does not deal with all the questions referred, the court may, if it thinks fit, either postpone the enforcement of the award or order its enforcement subject to the giving of such security by the person seeking to enforce it as the court may think fit.

(3) If a party seeking to resist the enforcement of a foreign award proves that there is any ground other than the non-existence of the conditions specified in paragraphs (a), (b) and (c) of subsection (1) of this section, or the existence of the conditions specified in paragraphs (b) and (c) of subsection (2) of this section, entitling him to contest the validity of the award, the court may, if it thinks fit, either refuse to enforce the award or adjourn the hearing until after the expiration of such period as appears to the court to be reasonably sufficient to enable that party to take the necessary steps to have the award annulled by the competent tribunal.

Evidence.   **38.**—(1) The party seeking to enforce a foreign award must produce—

(a) the original award or a copy thereof duly authenticated in manner required by the law of the country in which it was made ; and

(b) evidence proving that the award has become final ; and

(c) such evidence as may be necessary to prove that the award is a foreign award and that the conditions mentioned in paragraphs (a), (b) and (c) of subsection (1) of the last foregoing section are satisfied.

(2) In any case where any document required to be produced under subsection (1) of this section is in a foreign language, it shall be the duty of the party seeking to enforce the award to produce a translation certified as correct by a diplomatic or consular agent of the country to which that party belongs, or certified as correct in such other manner as may be sufficient according to the law of England.

(3) Subject to the provisions of this section, rules of court may be made under section ninety-nine of the Supreme Court of Judicature (Consolidation) Act, 1925, with respect to the evidence which must be furnished by a party seeking to enforce an award under this Part of this Act.

39. For the purposes of this Part of this Act, an award shall not be deemed final if any proceedings for the purpose of contesting the validity of the award are pending in the country in which it was made.

PART II
—*cont.*

Meaning of
" final award ".

40. Nothing in this Part of this Act shall—

    (*a*) prejudice any rights which any person would have had of enforcing in England any award or of availing himself in England of any award if neither this Part of this Act nor Part I of the Arbitration (Foreign Awards) Act. 1930, had been enacted ; or

    (*b*) apply to any award made on an arbitration agreement governed by the law of England.

Saving for
other rights,
&c.

41.—(1) The following provisions of this section shall have effect for the purpose of the application of this Part of this Act to Scotland.

Application of
Part II to
Scotland.

(2) For the references to England there shall be substituted references to Scotland.

(3) For subsection (1) of section thirty-six there shall be substituted the following subsection :—

    " (1) A foreign award shall, subject to the provisions of this Part of this Act, be enforceable by action, or, if the agreement for arbitration contains consent to the registration of the award in the Books of Council and Session for execution and the award is so registered, it shall, subject as aforesaid, be enforceable by summary diligence ".

(4) For subsection (3) of section thirty-eight there shall be substituted the following subsection : —

    " (3) The Court of Session shall, subject to the provisions of this section, have power, exercisable by statutory instrument, to make provision by Act of Sederunt with respect to the evidence which must be furnished by a party seeking to enforce in Scotland an award under this Part of this Act, and the Statutory Instruments Act, 1946, shall apply to a statutory instrument containing an Act of Sederunt made under this subsection as if the Act of Sederunt had been made by a Minister of the Crown ".

42.—(1) The following provisions of this section shall have effect for the purpose of the application of this Part of this Act to Northern Ireland.

Application of
Part II to
Northern
Ireland.

(2) For the references to England there shall be substituted references to Northern Ireland.

PART II   (3) For subsection (1) of section thirty-six there shall be
—*cont.*   substituted the following subsection : —

" (1) A foreign award shall, subject to the provisions of this Part of this Act, be enforceable either by action or in the same manner as the award of an arbitrator under the provisions of the Common Law Procedure Amendment Act (Ireland), 1856, was enforceable at the date of the passing of the Arbitration (Foreign Awards) Act, 1930 ".

(4) For the reference, in subsection (3) of section thirty-eight. to section ninety-nine of the Supreme Court of Judicature (Consolidation) Act, 1925, there shall be substituted a reference to section sixty-one of the Supreme Court of Judicature (Ireland) Act, 1877, as amended by any subsequent enactment.

Saving for   **43.** * Any proceedings instituted under Part I of the Arbitration
pending   (Foreign Awards) Act, 1930, which are uncompleted at the
proceedings.   commencement of this Act may be carried on and completed under this Part of this Act as if they had been instituted thereunder.

PART III

GENERAL

Short title,   **44.**—(1) This Act may be cited as the Arbitration Act, 1950.
commencement
and repeal.   (2) This Act shall come into operation on the first day of September, nineteen hundred and fifty.

(3) The Arbitration Act, 1889, the Arbitration Clauses (Protocol) Act, 1924, and the Arbitration Act, 1934, are hereby repealed except in relation to arbitrations commenced (within the meaning of subsection (2) of section twenty-nine of this Act) before the commencement of this Act, and the Arbitration (Foreign Awards) Act, 1930, is hereby repealed ; and any reference in any Act or other document to any enactment hereby repealed shall be construed as including a reference to the corresponding provision of this Act.

* Section 43 repealed by the Statute Law (Revision) Act 1978.

SCHEDULES

FIRST SCHEDULE   Sections 4, 35.

PROTOCOL ON ARBITRATION CLAUSES SIGNED ON BEHALF OF HIS MAJESTY AT A MEETING OF THE ASSEMBLY OF THE LEAGUE OF NATIONS HELD ON THE TWENTY-FOURTH DAY OF SEPTEMBER, NINETEEN HUNDRED AND TWENTY-THREE

The undersigned, being duly authorised, declare that they accept, on behalf of the countries which they represent, the following provisions: —

1. Each of the Contracting States recognises the validity of an agreement whether relating to existing or future differences between parties, subject respectively to the jurisdiction of different Contracting States by which the parties to a contract agree to submit to arbitration all or any differences that may arise in connection with such contract relating to commercial matters or to any other matter capable of settlement by arbitration, whether or not the arbitration is to take place in a country to whose jurisdiction none of the parties is subject.

Each Contracting State reserves the right to limit the obligation mentioned above to contracts which are considered as commercial under its national law.   Any Contracting State which avails itself of this right will notify the Secretary-General of the League of Nations, in order that the other Contracting States may be so informed.

2. The arbitral procedure, including the constitution of the arbitral tribunal, shall be governed by the will of the parties and by the law of the country in whose territory the arbitration takes place.

The Contracting States agree to facilitate all steps in the procedure which require to be taken in their own territories, in accordance with the provisions of their law governing arbitral procedure applicable to existing differences.

3. Each Contracting State undertakes to ensure the execution by its authorities and in accordance with the provisions of its national laws of arbitral awards made in its own territory under the preceding articles.

4. The tribunals of the Contracting Parties, on being seized of a dispute regarding a contract made between persons to whom Article 1 applies and including an arbitration agreement whether referring to present or future differences which is valid in virtue of the said article and capable of being carried into effect, shall refer the parties on the application of either of them to the decision of the arbitrators.

Such reference shall not prejudice the competence of the judicial tribunals in case the agreement or the arbitration cannot proceed or become inoperative.

5. The present Protocol, which shall remain open for signature by all States, shall be ratified.   The ratifications shall be deposited as soon as possible with the Secretary-General of the League of Nations. who shall notify such deposit to all the signatory States.

6. The present Protocol shall come into force as soon as two ratifications have been deposited. Thereafter it will take effect, in the case of each Contracting State, one month after the notification by the Secretary-General of the deposit of its ratification.

7. The present Protocol may be denounced by any Contracting State on giving one year's notice. Denunciation shall be effected by a notification addressed to the Secretary-General of the League, who will immediately transmit copies of such notification to all the other signatory States and inform them of the date of which it was received. The denunciation shall take effect one year after the date on which it was notified to the Secretary-General, and shall operate only in respect of the notifying State.

8. The Contracting States may declare that their acceptance of the present Protocol does not include any or all of the under-mentioned territories: that is to say, their colonies, overseas possessions or territories, protectorates or the territories over which they exercise a mandate.

The said States may subsequently adhere separately on behalf of any territory thus excluded. The Secretary-General of the League of Nations shall be informed as soon as possible of such adhesions. He shall notify such adhesions to all signatory States. They will take effect one month after the notification by the Secretary-General to all signatory States.

The Contracting States may also denounce the Protocol separately on behalf of any of the territories referred to above. Article 7 applies to such denunciation.

SECOND SCHEDULE

CONVENTION ON THE EXECUTION OF FOREIGN ARBITRAL AWARDS SIGNED AT GENEVA ON BEHALF OF HIS MAJESTY ON THE TWENTY-SIXTH DAY OF SEPTEMBER, NINETEEN HUNDRED AND TWENTY-SEVEN

ARTICLE I

In the territories of any High Contracting Party to which the present Convention applies, an arbitral award made in pursuance of an agreement, whether relating to existing or future differences (hereinafter called " a submission to arbitration ") covered by the Protocol on Arbitration Clauses, opened at Geneva on September 24, 1923, shall be recognised as binding and shall be enforced in accordance with the rules of the procedure of the territory where the award is relied upon, provided that the said award has been made in a territory of one of the High Contracting Parties to which the present Convention applies and between persons who are subject to the jurisdiction of one of the High Contracting Parties.

To obtain such recognition or enforcement, it shall, further, be necessary: —

    (a) That the award has been made in pursuance of a submission to arbitration which is valid under the law applicable thereto ;

(b) That the subject-matter of the award is capable of settlement by arbitration under the law of the country in which the award is sought to be relied upon ;

(c) That the award has been made by the Arbitral Tribunal provided for in the submission to arbitration or constituted in the manner agreed upon by the parties and in conformity with the law governing the arbitration procedure ;

(d) That the award has become final in the country in which it has been made, in the sense that it will not be considered as such if it is open to *opposition, appel* or *pourvoi en cassation* (in the countries where such forms of procedure exist) or if it is proved that any proceedings for the purpose of contesting the validity of the award are pending ;

(e) That the recognition or enforcement of the award is not contrary to the public policy or to the principles of the law of the country in which it is sought to be relied upon.

ARTICLE 2

Even if the conditions laid down in Article 1 hereof are fulfilled, recognition and enforcement of the award shall be refused if the Court is satisfied : —

(a) That the award has been annulled in the country in which it was made ;

(b) That the party against whom it is sought to use the award was not given notice of the arbitration proceedings in sufficient time to enable him to present his case ; or that, being under a legal incapacity, he was not properly represented ;

(c) That the award does not deal with the differences contemplated by or falling within the terms of the submission to arbitration or that it contains decisions on matters beyond the scope of the submission to arbitration.

If the award has not covered all the questions submitted to the arbitral tribunal, the competent authority of the country where recognition or enforcement of the award is sought can, if it think fit, postpone such recognition or enforcement or grant it subject to such guarantee as that authority may decide.

ARTICLE 3

If the party against whom the award has been made proves that, under the law governing the arbitration procedure, there is a ground, other than the grounds referred to in Article 1 (a) and (c), and Article 2 (b) and (c), entitling him to contest the validity of the award in a Court of Law, the Court may, if it thinks fit, either refuse recognition or enforcement of the award or adjourn the consideration thereof, giving such party a reasonable time within which to have the award annulled by the competent tribunal.

ARTICLE 4

The party relying upon an award or claiming its enforcement must supply, in particular: —

 (1) The original award or a copy thereof duly authenticated, according to the requirements of the law of the country in which it was made ;

 (2) Documentary or other evidence to prove that the award has become final, in the sense defined in Article 1 (*d*), in the country in which it was made ;

 (3) When necessary, documentary or other evidence to prove that the conditions laid down in Article 1, paragraph 1 and paragraph 2 (*a*) and (*c*), have been fulfilled.

A translation of the award and of the other documents mentioned in this Article into the official language of the country where the award is sought to be relied upon may be demanded. Such translation must be certified correct by a diplomatic or consular agent of the country to which the party who seeks to rely upon the award belongs or by a sworn translator of the country where the award is sought to be relied upon.

ARTICLE 5

The provisions of the above Articles shall not deprive any interested party of the right of availing himself of an arbitral award in the manner and to the extent allowed by the law or the treaties of the country where such award is sought to be relied upon.

ARTICLE 6

The present Convention applies only to arbitral awards made after the coming into force of the Protocol on Arbitration Clauses, opened at Geneva on September 24th, 1923.

ARTICLE 7

The present Convention, which will remain open to the signature of all the signatories of the Protocol of 1923 on Arbitration Clauses, shall be ratified.

It may be ratified only on behalf of those Members of the League of Nations and non-Member States on whose behalf the Protocol of 1923 shall have been ratified.

Ratifications shall be deposited as soon as possible with the Secretary-General of the League of Nations, who will notify such deposit to all the signatories.

ARTICLE 8

The present Convention shall come into force three months after it shall have been ratified on behalf of two High Contracting Parties. Thereafter, it shall take effect, in the case of each High Contracting Party, three months after the deposit of the ratification on its behalf with the Secretary-General of the League of Nations.

ARTICLE 9

The present Convention may be denounced on behalf of any Member of the League or non-Member State. Denunciation shall be notified in writing to the Secretary-General of the League of Nations, who will immediately send a copy thereof, certified to be in conformity with the notification, to all the other Contracting Parties, at the same time informing them of the date on which he received it.

The denunciation shall come into force only in respect of the High Contracting Party which shall have notified it and one year after such notification shall have reached the Secretary-General of the League of Nations.

The denunciation of the Protocol on Arbitration Clauses shall entail, ipso facto, the denunciation of the present Convention.

ARTICLE 10

The present Convention does not apply to the Colonies, Protectorates or territories under suzerainty or mandate of any High Contracting Party unless they are specially mentioned.

The application of this Convention to one or more of such Colonies, Protectorates or territories to which the Protocol on Arbitration Clauses, opened at Geneva on September 24th, 1923, applies, can be effected at any time by means of a declaration addressed to the Secretary-General of the League of Nations by one of the High Contracting Parties.

Such declaration shall take effect three months after the deposit thereof.

The High Contracting Parties can at any time denounce the Convention for all or any of the Colonies, Protectorates or territories referred to above. Article 9 hereof applies to such denunciation.

ARTICLE 11

A certified copy of the present Convention shall be transmitted by the Secretary-General of the League of Nations to every Member of the League of Nations and to every non-Member State which signs the same.

Table of Statutes referred to in this Act

Short Title	Session and Chapter
Common Law Procedure Amendment Act (Ireland), 1856 ...	19 & 20 Vict. c. 102.
Supreme Court of Judicature (Ireland) Act, 1877	40 & 41 Vict. c. 57.
Arbitration Act, 1889	52 & 53 Vict. c. 49.
Merchant Shipping Act, 1894	57 & 58 Vict. c. 60.
Arbitration Clauses (Protocol) Act, 1924 ...	14 & 15 Geo. 5. c. 39.
Supreme Court of Judicature (Consolidation) Act, 1925 ...	15 & 16 Geo. 5. c. 49.
Arbitration (Foreign Awards) Act, 1930 ...	20 Geo. 5. c. 15.
Arbitration Act, 1934	24 & 25 Geo. 5. c. 14.
Statutory Instruments Act, 1946 ...	9 & 10 Geo. 6. c. 36.

Arbitration Act 1979

1979 CHAPTER 42

An Act to amend the law relating to arbitrations and for purposes connected therewith. [4th April 1979]

B E IT ENACTED by the Queen's most Excellent Majesty, by and with the advice and consent of the Lords Spiritual and Temporal, and Commons, in this present Parliament assembled, and by the authority of the same, as follows:—

1.—(1) In the Arbitration Act 1950 (in this Act referred to as "the principal Act") section 21 (statement of case for a decision of the High Court) shall cease to have effect and, without prejudice to the right of appeal conferred by subsection (2) below, the High Court shall not have jurisdiction to set aside or remit an award on an arbitration agreement on the ground of errors of fact or law on the face of the award.

Judicial review of arbitration awards. *1950 c. 27.*

(2) Subject to subsection (3) below, an appeal shall lie to the High Court on any question of law arising out of an award made on an arbitration agreement; and on the determination of such an appeal the High Court may by order—

(a) confirm, vary or set aside the award; or

(b) remit the award to the reconsideration of the arbitrator or umpire together with the court's opinion on the question of law which was the subject of the appeal;

and where the award is remitted under paragraph (b) above the arbitrator or umpire shall, unless the order otherwise directs, make his award within three months after the date of the order.

(3) An appeal under this section may be brought by any of the parties to the reference—

 (a) with the consent of all the other parties to the reference ; or

 (b) subject to section 3 below, with the leave of the court.

(4) The High Court shall not grant leave under subsection (3)(b) above unless it considers that, having regard to all the circumstances, the determination of the question of law concerned could substantially affect the rights of one or more of the parties to the arbitration agreement ; and the court may make any leave which it gives conditional upon the applicant complying with such conditions as it considers appropriate.

(5) Subject to subsection (6) below, if an award is made and, on an application made by any of the parties to the reference,—

 (a) with the consent of all the other parties to the reference, or

 (b) subject to section 3 below, with the leave of the court,

it appears to the High Court that the award does not or does not sufficiently set out the reasons for the award, the court may order the arbitrator or umpire concerned to state the reasons for his award in sufficient detail to enable the court, should an appeal be brought under this section, to consider any question of law arising out of the award.

(6) In any case where an award is made without any reason being given, the High Court shall not make an order under subsection (5) above unless it is satisfied—

 (a) that before the award was made one of the parties to the reference gave notice to the arbitrator or umpire concerned that a reasoned award would be required ; or

 (b) that there is some special reason why such a notice was not given.

The following was added by s. 148(2) Supreme Court Act 1981:

(6A) Unless the High Court gives leave, the appeal shall lie to the Court of Appeal from a decision of the High Court—

 (a) to grant or refuse leave under subsection 3(b) or 5(b) above; or

 (b) to make or not to make an order under subsection 5 above.

(7) No appeal shall lie to the Court of Appeal from a decision of the High Court on an appeal under this section unless—

 (a) the High Court or the Court of Appeal gives leave ; and

 (b) it is certified by the High Court that the question of law to which its decision relates either is one of general public importance or is one which for some other special reason should be considered by the Court of Appeal.

(8) Where the award of an arbitrator or umpire is varied on appeal, the award as varied shall have effect (except for the purposes of this section) as if it were the award of the arbitrator or umpire.

2.—(1) Subject to subsection (2) and section 3 below, on an application to the High Court made by any of the parties to a reference— *Determination of preliminary point of law by court.*

    (a) with the consent of an arbitrator who has entered on the reference or, if an umpire has entered on the reference, with his consent, or

    (b) with the consent of all the other parties,

the High Court shall have jurisdiction to determine any question of law arising in the course of the reference.

(2) The High Court shall not entertain an application under subsection (1)(a) above with respect to any question of law unless it is satisfied that—

    (a) the determination of the application might produce substantial savings in costs to the parties; and

    (b) the question of law is one in respect of which leave to appeal would be likely to be given under section 1(3)(b) above.

The following was added by s. 148 Supreme Court Act 1981: (2A) Unless the High Court gives leave, no appeal shall lie to the Court of Appeal from a decision of the High Court to entertain or not to entertain an application under subsection 1(a) above.

(3)* A decision of the High Court under this section shall be deemed to be a judgment of the court within the meaning of section 27 of the Supreme Court of Judicature (Consolidation) Act 1925 (appeals to the Court of Appeal), but no appeal shall lie from such a decision unless— *1925 c. 49.*

    (a) the High Court or the Court of Appeal gives leave; and

    (b) it is certified by the High Court that the question of law to which its decision relates either is one of general public importance or is one which for some other special reason should be considered by the Court of Appeal.

3.—(1) Subject to the following provisions of this section and section 4 below— *Exclusion agreements affecting rights under sections 1 and 2.*

    (a) the High Court shall not, under section 1(3)(b) above, grant leave to appeal with respect to a question of law arising out of an award, and

* Subsection (3) was substituted by the Supreme Court Act 1981, s. 148(3) to read: (3) A decision of the High Court under subsection (1) above shall be deemed to be a judgment of the court within the meaning of section 16 of the Supreme Court Act 1981 (appeals to the Court of Appeal), but no appeal shall lie from such a decision unless—

(*b*) the High Court shall not, under section 1(5)(*b*) above, grant leave to make an application with respect to an award, and

(*c*) no application may be made under section 2(1)(*a*) above with respect to a question of law,

if the parties to the reference in question have entered into an agreement in writing (in this section referred to as an " exclusion agreement ") which excludes the right of appeal under section 1 above in relation to that award or, in a case falling within paragraph (*c*) above, in relation to an award to which the determination of the question of law is material.

(2) An exclusion agreement may be expressed so as to relate to a particular award, to awards under a particular reference or to any other description of awards, whether arising out of the same reference or not ; and an agreement may be an exclusion agreement for the purposes of this section whether it is entered into before or after the passing of this Act and whether or not it forms part of an arbitration agreement.

(3) In any case where—

(*a*) an arbitration agreement, other than a domestic arbitration agreement, provides for disputes between the parties to be referred to arbitration, and

(*b*) a dispute to which the agreement relates involves the question whether a party has been guilty of fraud, and

(*c*) the parties have entered into an exclusion agreement which is applicable to any award made on the reference of that dispute,

then, except in so far as the exclusion agreement otherwise provides, the High Court shall not exercise its powers under section 24(2) of the principal Act (to take steps necessary to enable the question to be determined by the High Court) in relation to that dispute.

(4) Except as provided by subsection (1) above, sections 1 and 2 above shall have effect notwithstanding anything in any agreement purporting—

(*a*) to prohibit or restrict access to the High Court ; or

(*b*) to restrict the jurisdiction of that court ; or

(*c*) to prohibit or restrict the making of a reasoned award.

(5) An exclusion agreement shall be of no effect in relation to an award made on, or a question of law arising in the course of a reference under, a statutory arbitration, that is to say, such an arbitration as is referred to in subsection (1) of section 31 of the principal Act.

(6) An exclusion agreement shall be of no effect in relation to an award made on, or a question of law arising in the course of a reference under, an arbitration agreement which is a domestic arbitration agreement unless the exclusion agreement is entered into after the commencement of the arbitration in which the award is made or, as the case may be, in which the question of law arises.

(7) In this section " domestic arbitration agreement " means an arbitration agreement which does not provide, expressly or by implication, for arbitration in a State other than the United Kingdom and to which neither—

    (a) an individual who is a national of, or habitually resident in, any State other than the United Kingdom, nor

    (b) a body corporate which is incorporated in, or whose central management and control is exercised in, any State other than the United Kingdom,

is a party at the time the arbitration agreement is entered into.

4.—(1) Subject to subsection (3) below, if an arbitration award or a question of law arising in the course of a reference relates, in whole or in part, to— *(Exclusion agreements not to apply in certain cases.)*

    (a) a question or claim falling within the Admiralty jurisdiction of the High Court, or

    (b) a dispute arising out of a contract of insurance, or

    (c) a dispute arising out of a commodity contract,

an exclusion agreement shall have no effect in relation to the award or question unless either—

    (i) the exclusion agreement is entered into after the commencement of the arbitration in which the award is made or, as the case may be, in which the question of law arises, or

    (ii) the award or question relates to a contract which is expressed to be governed by a law other than the law of England and Wales.

(2) In subsection (1)(c) above " commodity contract " means a contract—

    (a) for the sale of goods regularly dealt with on a commodity market or exchange in England or Wales which is specified for the purposes of this section by an order made by the Secretary of State ; and

    (b) of a description so specified.

(3) The Secretary of State may by order provide that subsection (1) above—

    (a) shall cease to have effect ; or

    (b) subject to such conditions as may be specified in the order, shall not apply to any exclusion agreement made in relation to an arbitration award of a description so specified ,

and an order under this subsection may contain such supplementary, incidental and transitional provisions as appear to the Secretary of State to be necessary or expedient.

(4) The power to make an order under subsection (2) or subsection (3) above shall be exercisable by statutory instrument which shall be subject to annulment in pursuance of a resolution of either House of Parliament.

(5) In this section "exclusion agreement" has the same meaning as in section 3 above.

Interlocutory orders.

5.—(1) If any party to a reference under an arbitration agreement fails within the time specified in the order or, if no time is so specified, within a reasonable time to comply with an order made by the arbitrator or umpire in the course of the reference, then, on the application of the arbitrator or umpire or of any party to the reference, the High Court may make an order extending the powers of the arbitrator or umpire as mentioned in subsection (2) below.

(2) If an order is made by the High Court under this section, the arbitrator or umpire shall have power, to the extent and subject to any conditions specified in that order, to continue with the reference in default of appearance or of any other act by one of the parties in like manner as a judge of the High Court might continue with proceedings in that court where a party fails to comply with an order of that court or a requirement of rules of court.

1970 c. 31.

(3) Section 4(5) of the Administration of Justice Act 1970 (jurisdiction of the High Court to be exercisable by the Court of Appeal in relation to judge-arbitrators and judge-umpires) shall not apply in relation to the power of the High Court to make an order under this section, but in the case of a reference to a judge-arbitrator or judge-umpire that power shall be exercisable as in the case of any other reference to arbitration and also by the judge-arbitrator or judge-umpire himself.

(4) Anything done by a judge-arbitrator or judge-umpire in the exercise of the power conferred by subsection (3) above shall be done by him in his capacity as judge of the High Court and have effect as if done by that court.

(5) The preceding provisions of this section have effect notwithstanding anything in any agreement but do not derogate from any powers conferred on an arbitrator or umpire, whether by an arbitration agreement or otherwise.

(6) In this section "judge-arbitrator" and "judge-umpire" have the same meaning as in Schedule 3 to the Administration of Justice Act 1970.

Minor amendments relating to awards and appointment of arbitrators and umpires.

6.—(1) In subsection (1) of section 8 of the principal Act (agreements where reference is to two arbitrators deemed to include provision that the arbitrators shall appoint an umpire immediately after their own appointment)—

(a) for the words " shall appoint an umpire immediately " there shall be substituted the words " may appoint an umpire at any time " ; and

(b) at the end there shall be added the words " and shall do so forthwith if they cannot agree ".

(2) For section 9 of the principal Act (agreements for reference to three arbitrators) there shall be substituted the following section:—

"Majority award of three arbitrators.   9. Unless the contrary intention is expressed in the arbitration agreement, in any case where there is a reference to three arbitrators, the award of any two of the arbitrators shall be binding."

(3) In section 10 of the principal Act (power of court in certain cases to appoint an arbitrator or umpire) in paragraph (c) after the word "are", in the first place where it occurs, there shall be inserted the words "required or are" and the words from "or where" to the end of the paragraph shall be omitted.

(4) At the end of section 10 of the principal Act there shall be added the following subsection:—

"(2) In any case where—

(a) an arbitration agreement provides for the appointment of an arbitrator or umpire by a person who is neither one of the parties nor an existing arbitrator (whether the provision applies directly or in default of agreement by the parties or otherwise), and

(b) that person refuses to make the appointment or does not make it within the time specified in the agreement or, if no time is so specified, within a reasonable time,

any party to the agreement may serve the person in question with a written notice to appoint an arbitrator or umpire and, if the appointment is not made within seven clear days after the service of the notice, the High Court or a judge thereof may, on the application of the party who gave the notice, appoint an arbitrator or umpire who shall have the like powers to act in the reference and make an award as if he had been appointed in accordance with the terms of the agreement."

7.—(1) References in the following provisions of Part I of the principal Act to that Part of that Act shall have effect as if the preceding provisions of this Act were included in that Part, namely,— *Application and interpretation of certain provisions of Part I of principal Act.*

(a) section 14 (interim awards);

(b) section 28 (terms as to costs of orders);

(c) section 30 (Crown to be bound);

(d) section 31 (application to statutory arbitrations); and

(e) section 32 (meaning of "arbitration agreement").

(2) Subsections (2) and (3) of section 29 of the principal Act shall apply to determine when an arbitration is deemed to be commenced for the purposes of this Act.

(3) For the avoidance of doubt, it is hereby declared that the reference in subsection (1) of section 31 of the principal Act (statutory arbitrations) to arbitration under any other Act does not extend to arbitration under section 92 of the County Courts Act 1959 (cases in which proceedings are to be or may be referred to arbitration) and accordingly nothing in this Act or in Part I of the principal Act applies to arbitration under the said section 92.

1959 c. 22.

Short title, commencement, repeals and extent.

8.—(1) This Act may be cited as the Arbitration Act 1979.

(2) This Act shall come into operation on such day as the Secretary of State may appoint by order made by statutory instrument ; and such an order—

(a) may appoint different days for different provisions of this Act and for the purposes of the operation of the same provision in relation to different descriptions of arbitration agreement ; and

(b) may contain such supplementary, incidental and transitional provisions as appear to the Secretary of State to be necessary or expedient.

(3) In consequence of the preceding provisions of this Act, the following provisions are hereby repealed, namely--

(a) in paragraph (c) of section 10 of the principal Act the words from " or where " to the end of the paragraph ;

(b) section 21 of the principal Act ;

1970 c. 31.

(c) in paragraph 9 of Schedule 3 to the Administration of Justice Act 1970, in sub-paragraph (1) the words " 21(1) and (2) " and sub-paragraph (2).

(4) This Act forms part of the law of England and Wales only.

Arbitration Rules of the Chartered Institute of Arbitrators (1988 edition)

Set out below are the Arbitration Rules of the Chartered Institute of Arbitrators, adopted to take effect from 1st January 1988. Earlier editions of these rules, particularly the edition adopted in and operative from 1981, are in frequent use, having been referred to in the arbitration clause of the original agreement under which the dispute has arisen; or adopted *ad hoc* by agreement of the parties.

The 1988 rules therefore are more likely to be used in cases arising in the future either because contracts henceforth refer to them or because the parties adopt them at the invitation of the arbitrator or otherwise.

Article 1 of the rules is, of course, optional, and deals with a case in which the claimant approaches the Institute for guidance in the first instance; more frequently, however, the rules are not invoked until the arbitrator has been appointed and invites the agreement of the parties to the adoption of the rules, whereupon Article 4 *et seq.* will apply.

The booklet published by the Chartered Institute of Arbitrators comprising the rules includes a note which makes it plain that these rules 'are not intended for use in arbitrations relating to international contracts or disputes (i.e. where the parties come from different countries). In such cases, reference should be made to the rules of the London Court of International Arbitration.'

(The rules of the London Court follow these rules on page 100.)

SUGGESTED CLAUSES

1. Parties to a contract who wish to have any *future* disputes referred to arbitration under the Rules of the Chartered Institute of Arbitrators may insert in the contract an arbitration clause in the following form:

   'Any dispute arising out of or in connection with this contract shall be referred to and finally resolved by arbitration under the Rules of the Chartered Institute of Arbitrators, which Rules are deemed to be incorporated by reference into this clause.'

2. Parties to an *existing* dispute who wish to refer it to arbitration under the Rules of the Chartered Institute of Arbitrators may agree to do so in the following terms:

   'We, the undersigned, agree to refer to arbitration under the Rules of the Chartered Institute of Arbitrators the following dispute which has arisen between us:

   (Brief description of matters to be referred to arbitration)

   Signed _____(Claimant)
   Signed _____ (Respondent)
   Date _____

3. Where the Rules of the Chartered Institute of Arbitrators apply:

   (a) The parties may if they wish specify an Appointing Authority to appoint the arbitrator (or arbitrators) if the parties fail to do so or cannot agree. If no Appointing Authority is specified, then the Rules provide the President or a Vice-President for the time being of the Chartered Institute of Arbitrators will act as Appointing Authority. The following provision may be suitable if some other Appointing Authority is required:

      'The Appointing Authority shall be (name of institution or person).'

   (b) The Rules provide a sole arbitrator will be appointed unless the parties agree otherwise. If the parties wish to specify a three-man tribunal, the following provision may be suitable:

      'The arbitral tribunal shall consist of three arbitrators one of whom shall be appointed by each party and the third by the Appointing Authority.'

ARBITRATION RULES

Rules adopted to take effect from 1 January 1988

Where any agreement, submission or reference provides for arbitration under the Rules of the Chartered Institute of Arbitrators, the parties shall be taken to have agreed that the arbitration shall be conducted in accordance with the following Rules, or such amended Rules as the Chartered Institute of Arbitrators may have adopted to take effect before the commencement of the arbitration.

Article 1   Commencement of Arbitration

1.1   Any party wishing to commence an arbitration under these Rules ('the Claimant') shall send to the other party ('the Respondent') a written request for arbitration ('the Request') which shall include, or be accompanied by:

   (a) the names and addresses of the parties to the arbitration; ·

   (b) copies of the contractual documents in which the arbitration clause is contained or under which the arbitration arises;

   (c) a brief statement describing the nature and circumstances of the dispute, and specifying the relief claimed;

   (d) a statement of any matters (such as the Appointing Authority, the number of arbitrators, or their qualifications or identities) with respect to which the requesting party wishes to make a proposal;

   (e) if the arbitration agreement calls for each party to appoint an arbitrator, the name and address (and telephone, telex and fax numbers, if known) of the arbitrator appointed by the Claimant.

   The arbitration shall be deemed to commence on the date of receipt by the Respondent of the Request for Arbitration.

1.2   For the purpose of facilitating the choice of arbitrators, within 30 days of receipt of the

Request for Arbitration, the Respondent may send to the Claimant a Response containing:

(a) confirmation or denial of all or part of the claims;

(b) a brief statement of the nature and circumstances of any envisaged counterclaims;

(c) comment (including confirmation of agreement) in response to any proposals contained in the Request, as called for under Article 1.1(d), on matters relating to the conduct of the arbitration;

(d) if the arbitration agreement calls for each party to appoint an arbitrator, the name and address (and telephone, telex and fax numbers if known) of the arbitrator appointed by the Respondent.

1.3 Failure to send a Response shall not preclude the Respondent from denying the claim nor from setting out a counterclaim in its Statement of Defence. However, if the arbitration agreement calls for each party to appoint an arbitrator, failure to send a Response or to name an appointed arbitrator in it within the time specified in Article 1.2 shall constitute a waiver of the right to appoint an arbitrator.

Article 2   Appointing Authority

2.1 The parties may agree to nominate an Appointing Authority. Failing such nomination the Appointing Authority shall be the President or a Vice-President for the time being of the Chartered Institute of Arbitrators.

2.2 Any application to the Appointing Authority to act in accordance with these Rules shall be accompanied by:

(a) Copies of the Request and Response and any other related correspondence;

(b) Confirmation that a copy of the application has been received by the other party;

(c) Particulars of any method or criteria of selection of arbitrators agreed by the parties.

The Appointing Authority may require payment of a fee for its services.

Article 3   Appointment of Arbitrator

3.1 Provided that the final number is uneven, the parties may agree on the number of arbitrators in the Tribunal. Failing such agreement there shall be a sole arbitrator. In these Rules, the expression 'the Arbitrator' includes a sole arbitrator or all the arbitrators where more than one is appointed.

3.2 The Arbitrator shall be and remain at all times wholly independent and impartial, and shall not act as advocate for any party. Before appointment if so requested by either party or the Appointing Authority any proposed arbitrator shall furnish a resume of his past and present professional activities (which will be communicated to the parties). In any event any arbitrator if so requested by either party or the Appointing Authority shall sign a declaration to the effect that there are no circumstances likely to give rise to any justified doubts as to his impartiality or independence, and that he will forthwith disclose any such circumstances to the parties if they should arise after that time and before the arbitration is concluded.

3.3 The Arbitrator may be appointed by agreement of the parties. Failing such agreement within 30 days of the commencement of the arbitration in accordance with Article 1, the Arbitrator shall upon the application of either party be appointed by the Appointing Authority.

3.4 Where the parties have agreed there shall be three arbitrators, they may also agree that each party shall appoint an arbitrator. If either party fails to make and notify the other party of such appointment within 30 days of the commencement of the arbitration under Article 1, that appointment shall be made by the Appointing Authority.

3.5 Where the parties have agreed that each shall appoint an arbitrator then, unless otherwise agreed by the parties, a third arbitrator shall be appointed by the Appointing Authority.

3.6 Where there are three or more arbitrators, they may agree who shall act as Chairman of the arbitral tribunal. Failing such agreement the Chairman shall be designated by the Appointing Authority.

3.7 If any arbitrator, after appointment, dies, is unable to act, or refuses to act, the Appointing Authority will, upon request by a party or by the remaining arbitrators, appoint another arbitrator.

Article 4 Communications between Parties and the Arbitrator

4.1 Where the Arbitrator sends any communication to one party, he shall send a copy to the other party.

4.2 Where a party sends any communication (including Statements under Article 6) to the Arbitrator, it shall be copied to the other party and be shown to the Arbitrator to have been so copied.

4.3 The addresses of the parties for the purpose of all communications during the proceedings shall be those set out in the Request, or as either party may at any time notify to the Arbitrator and to the other party. Any communication by post shall be deemed to be received in the ordinary course of mail unless the contrary is proved.

4.4 With the agreement of the parties, the Arbitrator may appoint the Registrar of the Chartered Institute of Arbitrators to act as arbitration administrator (whether or not the Chartered Institute of Arbitrators is acting as Appointing Authority). Where the Registrar is so appointed, all communications and notices between a party and the Arbitrator in the course of the arbitration (except at meetings and hearings) will be addressed through the Registrar, and in the case of communications to the Arbitrator will be deemed received by him when received by the Registrar.

Article 5 Conduct of the Proceedings

5.1 In the absence of procedural rules agreed by the parties or contained herein, the Arbitrator shall have the widest discretion allowed by law to ensure the just, expeditious, economical, and final determination of the dispute.

5.2 Any party wishing the Arbitrator to adopt a simplified or expedited procedure should apply to the Arbitrator for this within 15 days of notification of the Arbitrator's acceptance of his appointment.

5.3 In the case of a three-member tribunal the Chairman may, after consulting the other arbitrators, make procedural rulings alone.

Article 6 Submission of Written Statements and Documents

6.1 Subject to any procedural rules agreed by the parties or determined by or requested from the Arbitrator under Article 5, the written stage of the proceedings shall be as set out in this Article (and in accordance with Article 4).

6.2 Within 30 days of receipt by the Claimant of notification of the Arbitrator's acceptance of the appointment, the Claimant shall send to the Arbitrator a Statement of Case setting out in sufficient detail the facts and any contentions of law on which it relies and the relief claimed.

6.3 Within 30 days of receipt of the Statement of Case, the Respondent shall send to the Arbitrator a Statement of Defence stating in sufficient detail which of the facts and contentions of law in the Statement of Case it admits or denies, on what grounds, and on what other facts and contentions of law it relies. Any Counterclaims shall be submitted with the Statement of Defence in the same manner as claims are set out in the Statement of Case.

6.4 Within 30 days of receipt of the Statement of Defence, the Claimant may send to the Arbitrator a Statement of Reply which, where there are Counterclaims, shall include a Defence to Counterclaims.

6.5 If the Statement of Reply contains a Defence to Counterclaims, the Respondent may within a further 30 days send to the Arbitrator a Statement of Reply regarding Counterclaims.

6.6 All Statements referred to in this Article shall be accompanied by copies (or, if they are especially voluminous, lists) of all essential documents on which the party concerned relies and which have not previously been submitted by any party, and (where appropriate) by any relevant samples.

6.7 As soon as practicable following completion of the submission of the Statements specified in this Article, the Arbitrator shall proceed in such manner as has been agreed by the parties, or pursuant to his authority under these Rules.

Article 7 Party Representatives

Any party may be represented by persons of their choice, subject to such proof of authority as the Arbitrator may require. The names and addresses of such representatives must be notified to the other party.

Article 8   Hearings

8.1   Subject to Article 12, each party has the right to be heard before the Arbitrator, unless the parties have agreed to documents-only arbitration.

8.2   The Arbitrator shall fix the date, time and place of any meetings and hearings in the arbitration, and shall give the parties reasonable notice thereof.

8.3   The Arbitrator may in advance of hearings provide the parties with a list of matters or questions to which he wishes them to give special consideration.

8.4   All meetings and hearings shall be in private unless the parties agree otherwise.

Article 9   Witnesses

9.1   The Arbitrator may require each party to give notice of the identity of witnesses it intends to call. The Arbitrator may also require before a hearing the exchange of witnesses statements and of expert reports.

9.2   The Arbitrator has discretion to allow, limit, or (subject to Article 10.2) refuse to allow the appearance of witnesses, whether witnesses of fact or expert witnesses.

9.3   Any witness who gives oral evidence may be questioned by each party or its representative, under the control of the Arbitrator, and may be required by the Arbitrator to testify under oath or affirmation in accordance with the Arbitration Act 1950. The Arbitrator may put questions at any stage of the examination of the witnesses.

9.4   The testimony of witnesses may be presented in written form, either as signed statements or by duly sworn affidavits. Subject to Article 9.2 any party may request that such a witness should attend for oral examination at a hearing. If the witness fails to attend, the Arbitrator may place such weight on the written testimony as he thinks fit, or may exclude it altogether.

Article 10   Experts Appointed by the Arbitrator

10.1 Unless otherwise agreed by the parties, the Arbitrator:

(a) may appoint one or more experts to report to the Arbitrator on specific issues;

(b) may require a party to give any such expert any relevant information or to produce, or to provide access to, any relevant documents, goods or property for inspection by the expert.

10.2 Unless otherwise agreed by the parties, if a party so requests or if the Arbitrator considers it necessary, the expert shall, after delivery of his written or oral report, participate in a hearing, at which the parties shall have the opportunity to question him and to present expert witnesses in order to testify on the points at issue.

10.3 The provisions of Article 10.2 shall not apply to an assessor appointed by agreement of the parties, nor to an expert appointed by the Arbitrator to advise him solely in relation to procedural matters.

Article 11   Additional Powers of the Arbitrator

11.1 Unless the parties at any time agree otherwise, the Arbitrator shall have the power to:

(a) allow any party, upon such terms (as to costs and otherwise) as he shall determine, to amend claims or counterclaims;

(b) extend or abbreviate any time limits provided by these Rules or by his directions;

(c) conduct such enquiries as many appear to the Arbitrator to be necessary or expedient;

(d) order the parties to make any property or thing available for inspection, in their presence, by the Arbitrator or any expert;

(e) order any party to produce to the Arbitrator, and to the other parties for inspection, and to supply copies of any documents or classes of documents in their possession, custody or power which the Arbitrator determines to be relevant.

11.2 If the parties so agree the Arbitrator shall also have the power to:

(a) order the rectification in any contract or arbitration agreement of any mistake which he determines to be common to the parties;

(b) rule on the existence, validity or determination of the contract;

(c) rule on his own jurisdiction, including any objections with respect to the existence or validity of the arbitration agreement or to his terms of reference.

Article 12   Jurisdiction of the Arbitrator

12.1 In addition to the jurisdiction to exercise the powers defined elsewhere in these Rules, the Arbitrator shall have jurisdiction to:

(a) determine any question of law arising in the arbitration;

(b) receive and take into account such written or oral evidence as he shall determine to be relevant, whether or not strictly admissible in law;

(c) proceed in the arbitration and make an award notwithstanding the failure or refusal of any party to comply with these Rules or with the Arbitrator's written orders or written directions, or to exercise its right to present its case, but only after giving that party written notice that he intends to do so.

12.2 If the Claimant fails to attend any hearing of which due notice has been given, the Arbitrator may make an award on the substantive issue and an award as to costs, with or without a hearing, but such an award must be an Interim Award with the provision that it shall become a Final Award after 42 days if no application for a hearing is made by the Claimant during that period. If the Respondent fails to submit a Statement of Defence or to attend any hearing after due notice has been given, the Arbitrator may conduct the hearing in the absence of the Respondent and make an Award.

Article 13   Deposits and Security

13.1 The Arbitrator may direct the parties, in such proportions as he deems just, to make one or more deposits to secure the Arbitrator's fees and expenses. Such deposits shall be made to and held by the Arbitrator, or the Chartered Institute of Arbitrators or some other person or body to the order of the Arbitrator, as the Arbitrator may direct, and may be drawn from as required by the Arbitrator. Interest on sums deposited, if any, shall be accumulated to the deposits.

13.2 The Arbitrator shall have the power to order any party to provide security for the legal or other costs of any other party by way of deposit or bank guarantee or in any other manner the Arbitrator thinks fit.

13.3 The Arbitrator shall also have the power to order any party to provide security for all or part of any amount in dispute in the arbitration.

Article 14   The Award

14.1 The Arbitrator shall make his award in writing and, unless all the parties agree otherwise, shall state the reasons upon which his award is based. The award shall state its date and shall be signed by the Arbitrator.

14.2 Where there is more than one arbitrator and they fail to agree on any issue, they shall decide by a majority. Failing a majority decision on any issue, the Chairman of the tribunal shall make the award alone as if he were sole arbitrator. If an arbitrator refuses or fails to sign the award, the signatures of the majority shall be sufficient, provided that the reason for the omitted signature is stated.

14.3 The Arbitrator shall be responsible for delivering the award or certified copies thereof to the parties, provided that he has been paid his fees and expenses.

14.4 The Arbitrator may make interim awards or separate awards on different issues at different times.

14.5 If, before the award is made, the parties agree on a settlement of the dispute, the Arbitrator shall either issue an order for termination of the reference to arbitration or, if requested by both parties and accepted by the Arbitrator, record the settlement in the form of a consent award. The Arbitrator shall then be discharged and the reference to arbitration concluded, subject to payment by the parties of any outstanding fees and expenses of the Arbitrator.

Article 15   Correction of Awards and Additional Awards

15.1 Within 14 days of receiving an award, unless another period of time has been agreed upon by the parties, a party may by notice to the Arbitrator request the Arbitrator to correct in the award any errors in computation, any clerical or typographical errors or any errors of similar nature. If the Arbitrator considers the request to be justified, he shall make the corrections within 14 days of receiving the request. Any correction shall be notified in writing to the parties and shall become part of the award.

15.2 The Arbitrator may correct any error of the type

referred to in Article 15.1 on his own initiative within 14 days of the date of the award

15.3 Unless otherwise agreed by the parties, a party may request the Arbitrator, within 10 days of the date of the award, and with notice to the other party, to make an additional award as to claims presented in the reference to arbitration but not dealt with in the award. If the Arbitrator considers the request to be justified, he shall notify the parties within 7 days and shall make the additional award within 30 days.

15.4 The provisions of Article 14 shall apply to any correction of the award and to any additional award.

Article 16   Costs

16.1 The Arbitrator shall specify in the award the total amount of his fees and expenses, including the charges of the arbitration administrator (if any). Unless the parties shall agree otherwise after the dispute has arisen, the Arbitrator shall determine the proportions in which the parties shall pay such fees and expenses, provided that the parties will be jointly and severally liable to the Arbitrator for payment of all such fees and expenses until they have been paid in full. If the Arbitrator has determined that all or any of his fees and expenses shall be paid by any party other than a party which has already paid them to the Arbitrator, the latter party shall have the right to recover the appropriate amount from the former.

16.2 The Arbitrator has power to order in his award that all or a part of the legal or other costs of one party shall be paid by the other party. The Arbitrator also has power to tax these costs and may do so if requested by the parties.

16.3 If the Arbitration is abandoned, suspended or concluded, by agreement or otherwise, before the final award is made, the parties shall be jointly and severally liable to pay to the Arbitrator his fees and expenses as determined by him together with the charges of the arbitration administrator (if any).

Article 17   Exclusion of Liability

17.1 The Arbitrator, the Appointing Authority (and the arbitration administrator if any) shall not be liable to any party for any act or omission in connection with any arbitration conducted under these Rules,

save for the consequences of conscious and deliberate wrongdoing.

17.2 After the award has been made and the possibilities of correction and additional awards referred to in Article 15 have lapsed or been exhausted, the Arbitrator, the Appointing Authority (and the arbitration administrator if any) shall not be under any obligation to make any statement to any person about any matter concerning the arbitration, and no party shall seek to make any arbitrator or the Appointing Authority or the arbitration administrator a witness in any legal proceedings arising out of the arbitration.

Article 18   Waiver

A party which is aware of non-compliance with these Rules and yet proceeds with the arbitration without promptly stating its objection to such non-compliance, shall be deemed to have waived its right to object.

Arbitration Rules of the London Court of International Arbitration

(1985 edition)

London Court of
International Arbitration

RULES

adopted to take effect from
1 January 1985

Where any agreement, submission or reference provides for arbitration under the Rules of the London Court of International Arbitration* (the LCIA), the parties shall be taken to have agreed that the arbitration shall be conducted in accordance with the following Rules, or such amended Rules as the Court may have adopted to take effect before the commencement of the arbitration.

The Arbitration Court of the LCIA, in these Rules called "The Court", has the function of ensuring the application of the Rules.

Article 1   Request for Arbitration

Any party wishing to commence an arbitration under these Rules ('the Claimant') shall send to the Registrar of the Court ('the Registrar') a written request for arbitration ('the Request') which shall include, or be accompanied by:

(a) the names and addresses of the parties to the arbitration;

(b) copies of the contractual documents in which the arbitration clause is contained or under which the arbitration arises;

(c) a brief statement describing the nature and circumstances of the dispute, and specifying the relief claimed;

(d) a statement of any matters (such as the place or language of the arbitration, or the number of arbitrators, or their qualifications or identities) on which the parties have already agreed in relation to the conduct of the arbitration, or with respect to which the requesting party wishes to make a proposal;

*Formerly called the London Court of Arbitration

(e) if the arbitration agreement calls for party nomination of arbitrators, the name and address (and telephone and telex numbers, if known) of the Claimant's nominee;

(f) the fee prescribed in the Schedule of Costs;

and shall confirm to the Registrar that copies have been served on the other parties. The date of receipt by the Registrar of the Request for Arbitration shall be deemed to be the date on which the arbitration has commenced.

Article 2   Response by Respondent

2.1 For the purpose of facilitating the choice of arbitrators, within 30 days of receipt of its copy of the Request for Arbitration the Respondent may send to the Registrar a Response containing:

(a) confirmation or denial of all or part of the claims;

(b) a brief statement of the nature and circumstances of any envisaged counterclaims;

(c) comment in response to any statements contained in the Request, as called for under Article 1(d), on matters relating to the conduct of the arbitration;

(d) if the arbitration agreement calls for party nomination of arbitrators, the name and address (and telephone and telex numbers if known) of the Respondent's nominee;

and shall confirm to the Registrar that copies have been served on the other parties.

2.2 Failure to send a Response shall not preclude the Respondent from denying the claim nor from setting out a counterclaim in its Statement of Defence. However, if the arbitration agreement calls for party nomination of arbitrators, failure to send a Response or to nominate an arbitrator in it shall constitute a waiver of the opportunity to nominate an arbitrator.

Article 3   The Arbitral Tribunal

3.1 In these Rules, the expression 'the Tribunal' includes a sole arbitrator or all the arbitrators where more than one is appointed. All arbitrators (whether or not nominated by the parties) conducting an arbitration under these Rules shall be and remain at all times wholly independent and impartial, and shall not act as advocates for any party. Before appointment by the Court, if the Registrar so requests, any arbitrator shall furnish a resumé of his past and present professional positions (which will be communicated to the parties). In any event every arbitrator shall sign a declaration to the effect that there are no circumstances likely to give rise to any justified doubts as to his impartiality or independence, and that he will forthwith disclose any such circumstances to the Court and to all the parties if they should arise after that time and before the arbitration is concluded.

3.2 The Court will appoint the Tribunal to determine the dispute as soon as practicable after receipt by the Registrar of the Response, or after the expiry of 30 days following receipt by the Respondent of the Request if no Response is received, provided that the Registrar is satisfied that the Request has been properly served. A sole arbitrator will be appointed unless the parties have agreed otherwise, or unless the Court determines that in view of all the circumstances of the case a three-member tribunal is appropriate.

3.3 The Court alone is empowered to appoint arbitrators and such appointment will be made in the name of the Court by the President or any Vice President of the Court. The Court will appoint arbitrators with due regard for any particular method or criteria of selection agreed by the parties. In selecting arbitrators consideration will be given, so far as possible, to the nature of the contract, the nature and circumstances of the dispute, and the nationality, location and languages of the parties. Where the parties are of different nationalities, then unless they have agreed otherwise, sole arbitrators or chairmen are not to be appointed if they have the same nationality as any party (the nationality of parties being understood to include that of controlling shareholders or interests). If the parties have agreed that they are to nominate arbitrators themselves, or to allow two arbitrators, or a third party, to nominate an arbitrator , the Court may refuse to appoint such nominees if it determines that they are not suitable or independent or impartial. In the case of a three-member Tribunal the Court will designate the Chairman, who will not be a party-nominated arbitrator.

3.4 If the arbitration agreement calls for party nominations, and the Respondent fails to make such a nomination within the time limit established by Article 2, the Court will forthwith appoint an arbitrator in place of the arbitrator to be nominated by the Respondent. If the Request does not contain a nomination by the Claimant, and the Claimant fails to make such a nomination with the same time limit, the Court will likewise make that appointment.

3.5 In the event that the Court determines that a nominee is not suitable or independent or impartial, or if an appointed arbitrator is to be replaced, the Court shall have discretion to decide whether or not to follow the original nominating process. If it so decides any opportunity for renomination shall be waived if not exercised within 30 days, after which the Court shall appoint the replacement as soon as practicable.

3.6 If any arbitrator, after appointment, dies, refuses, or in the opinion of the Court becomes unable or unfit to act, the Court will, upon request by a party or by the remaining arbitrators, appoint another arbitrator in accordance with the provisions of Article 3.5. If in the opinion of the Court an arbitrator acts in manifest violation of these Rules, or does not conduct the proceedings with reasonable diligence, he will be considered unfit.

3.7 An arbitrator may be challenged if circumstances exist that give rise to justifiable doubts as to his impartiality or independence. A party may challenge an arbitrator it has nominated, or in whose appointment it has participated, only for reasons of which it becomes aware after the appointment has been made.

3.8 A party who intends to challenge an arbitrator shall, within fifteen days of the constitution of the Tribunal or after becoming aware of any circumstances referred to in Article 3.6 or 3.7, whichever is the later, send a written statement of the reasons for the challenge to the Court. Unless the challenged arbitrator withdraws or the other party agrees to the challenge within 15 days of receipt of the written statement of challenge, the Court shall decide on the challenge.

3.9 The decision of the Court with respect to all matters referred to in this Article shall be final. Such decisions are deemed to be administrative in nature, and the Court shall not be required to give reasons for them. To the extent permitted by the law of the place of arbitration the parties shall be taken to have waived any right of appeal in respect of any such

decisions to a court of law or other judicial authority. If such appeals remain possible due to mandatory provisions of the law of the place of arbitration, the Court shall, subject to the provisions of the applicable law, decide whether the arbitral proceedings are to continue notwithstanding an appeal.

Article 4 Communications between Parties and the Tribunal

4.1 Until the Tribunal is finally constituted and the Court determines that it would be appropriate for the parties and the Tribunal to communicate directly, all communications between parties and arbitrators shall be made through the Registrar. If and when the Court directs that communication shall take place directly between the Tribunal and the parties (with simultaneous copies to the Registrar) all further reference in these Rules to the Registrar shall thereafter be read as references to the Tribunal.

4.2 Where the Registrar, on behalf of the Tribunal, sends any communication to one party, he shall send a copy to each of the other parties.

4.3 Where any party sends any communication (including Statements under Article 6) to the Registrar, it shall include a copy for each arbitrator, and it shall also send copies to all the other parties and confirm to the Registrar in writing that it has done so.

4.4 The addresses of the parties for the purpose of all communications during the proceedings shall be those set out in the Request, or as any party may at any time notify to the Registrar and to the other parties.

Article 5 Conduct of the Proceedings

5.1 The parties may agree on the arbitral procedure, and are encouraged to do so.

5.2 In the absence of procedural rules agreed by the parties or contained herein, the Tribunal shall have the widest discretion allowed under such law as may be applicable to ensure the just, expeditious, economical, and final determination of the dispute.

5.3 In the case of a three-member tribunal the Chairman may, after consulting the other arbitrators, make procedural rulings alone.

Article 6 Submission of Written Statements and Documents

6.1 Subject to any procedural rules agreed by the parties or determined by the Tribunal under Article 5, the written stage of the proceedings shall be as set out in this Article.

6.2 Within 30 days of receipt of notification from the Court of the appointment of the Tribunal, the Claimant shall send to the Registrar a Statement of Case setting out in sufficient detail the facts and any contentions of law on which it relies, and the relief claimed.

6.3 Within 40 days of receipt of the Statement of Case, the Respondent shall send to the Registrar a Statement of Defence stating in sufficient detail which of the facts and contentions of law in the Statement of Case it admits or denies, on what grounds, and on what other facts and contentions of law it relies. Any counterclaims shall be submitted with the Statement of Defence in the same manner as claims are set out in the Statement of Case.

6.4 Within 40 days of receipt of the Statement of Defence, the Claimant may send to the Registrar a Statement of Reply which, where there are counterclaims, shall include a Defence to Counterclaims.

6.5 If the Statement of Reply contains a Defence to Counterclaims, the Respondent has a further 40 days to send to the Registrar a Statement of Reply regarding Counterclaims.

6.6 All Statements referred to in this Article shall be accompanied by copies (or, if they are especially voluminous, lists) of all essential documents on which the party concerned relies and which have not previously been submitted by any party, and (where appropriate) by any relevant samples.

6.7 As soon as practicable following completion of the submission of the Statements specified in this Article, the Tribunal shall proceed in such manner as has been agreed by the parties, or pursuant to its authority under these Rules. If the Respondent fails to submit a Statement of Defence, or if at any point any party fails to avail itself of the opportunity to present its case in the manner directed by the Tribunal, the Tribunal may nevertheless proceed with the arbitration and make the award.

Article 7 Place of Arbitration

7.1 The parties may choose the place of arbitration. Failing such a choice, the place of arbitration shall be London, unless the Tribunal determines in view of all the circumstances of the case that another place is more appropriate.

7.2 The Tribunal may hold hearings and meetings anywhere convenient, subject to the provisions of Article 10.2, and provided that the award shall be made at the place of arbitration.

Article 8 Language of Arbitration

8.1 The language(s) of the arbitration shall be that of the document(s) containing the arbitration agreement, unless the parties have agreed otherwise.

8.2 If a document is drawn up in a language other than the language(s) of the arbitration, and no translation of such document is submitted by the party producing the document, The Tribunal, or if the Tribunal has not been appointed the Court, may order that party to submit a translation in a form to be determined by the Tribunal or the Court.

Article 9 Party Representatives

Any party may be represented by legal practitioners or any other representatives, subject to such proof of authority as the Tribunal may require.

Article 10 Hearings

10.1 Any party has the right to be heard before the Tribunal, unless the parties have agreed on documents-only arbitration.

10.2 The Tribunal shall fix the date, time and place of any meetings and hearings in the arbitration, and the Registrar shall give the parties reasonable notice thereof.

10.3 The Tribunal may in advance of hearings submit to the parties a list of questions which it wishes them to treat with special attention.

10.4 All meetings and hearings shall be in private unless the parties agree otherwise.

Article 11 Witnesses

11.1 Before any hearing, the Tribunal may require any party to give notice of the identity of witnesses it wishes to call, as well as the subject matter of their testimony and its relevance to the issues.

11.2 The Tribunal has discretion to allow, refuse, or limit the appearance of witnesses, whether witnesses of fact or expert witnesses.

11.3 Any witness who gives oral evidence may be questioned by each of the parties or their legal practitioners, under the control of the Tribunal. The Tribunal may put questions at any stage of the examination of the witnesses.

11.4 The testimony of witnesses may be presented in written form, either as signed statements or by duly sworn affidavits. Subject to Article 11.2 any party may request that such a witness should attend for oral examination at a hearing. If he fails to attend, the Tribunal may place such weight on the written testimony as it thinks fit, or exclude it altogether.

11.5 Subject to the mandatory provisions of any applicable law it shall be proper for any party or its legal practitioners to interview any witness or potential witness prior to his appearance at any hearing.

Article 12 Experts Appointed by the Tribunal

12.1 Unless otherwise agreed by the parties, the Tribunal:

(a) may appoint one or more experts to report to the Tribunal on specific issues;

(b) may require a party to give any such expert any relevant information or to produce, or to provide access to, any relevant documents, goods or property for inspection by the expert.

12.2 Unless otherwise agreed by the parties, if a party so requests or if the Tribunal considers it necessary, the expert shall, after delivery of his written or oral report, participate in a hearing at which the parties shall have the opportunity to question him, and to present expert witnesses in order to testify on the points at issue.

Article 13 Additional Powers of the Tribunal

13.1 Unless the parties at any time agree otherwise, and subject to any mandatory limitations of any applicable law, the Tribunal shall have the power, on the application of any party or of its own motion, but in either case only after giving the parties a proper opportunity to state their views, to:

(a) determine what are the rules of law governing or applicable to any contract, or arbitration agreement or issue between the parties;

(b) order the correction of any such contract or arbitration agreement, but only to the extent required to rectify any mistake which it determines to be common to all the parties and then only if and to the extent to which the rules of law governing or applicable to the contract permit such correction;

(c) allow other parties to be joined in the arbitration with their express consent, and make a single final award determining all disputes between them;

(d) allow any party, upon such terms (as to costs and otherwise) as it shall determine, to amend claims or counterclaims;

(e) extend or abbreviate any time limits provided by these Rules or by its directions;

(f) conduct such enquiries as may appear to the Tribunal to be necessary or expedient;

(g) order the parties to make any property or thing available for inspection, in their presence, by the Tribunal or any expert;

(h) order the preservation, storage, sale or other disposal of any property or thing under the control of any party;

(i) order any party to produce to the Tribunal, and to the other parties for inspection, and to supply copies of, any documents or classes of documents in their possession or power which the Tribunal determines to be relevant.

13.2 By agreeing to arbitration under these Rules the parties shall be taken to have agreed to apply only to the Tribunal, and not to any court of law or other judicial authority, for an order under paragraphs (g), (h) or (i) of Article 13.1.

Article 14 Jurisdiction of the Tribunal

14.1 The Tribunal shall have the power to rule on its own jurisdiction, including any objections with respect to the existence or validity of the arbitration agreement. For that purpose, an arbitration clause which forms part of a contract shall be treated as an agreement independent of the other terms of the contract. A decision by the Tribunal that the contract is null and void shall not entail ipso jure the invalidity of the arbitration clause.

14.2 A plea that the Tribunal does not have jurisdiction shall be raised not later than in the Statement of Defence. A plea that the Tribunal is exceeding the scope of its authority shall be raised promptly after the Tribunal has indicated its intention to decide on the matter alleged to be beyond the scope of its authority. In either case the Tribunal may nevertheless admit a late plea under this paragraph if it considers the delay justified.

14.3 In addition to the jurisdiction to exercise the powers defined elsewhere in these Rules, the Tribunal shall have jurisdiction to determine any question of law arising in the arbitration; proceed in the arbitration notwithstanding the failure or refusal of any party to comply with these Rules or with the Tribunal's orders or directions, or to attend any meeting or hearing, but only after giving that party written notice that it intends to do so; and to receive and take into account such written or oral evidence as it shall determine to be relevant, whether or not strictly admissible in law.

Article 15 Deposits and Security

15.1 The Tribunal may direct the parties, in such proportions as it deems just, and subject to the confirmation of the Court that the amounts are in conformity with the Schedule of Costs, to make one or several interim or final payments on account of the costs of the arbitration. Such deposits shall be made to and held by the Court to the order of the Chairman of the Tribunal or sole arbitrator, and may be drawn from as required by the Tribunal. Interest on sums deposited, if any, shall be accumulated to the deposits.

15.2 The Tribunal shall have the power to order any party to provide security for the legal or other costs of any other party by way of deposit or bank guarantee or in any other manner the Tribunal thinks fit.

15.3 By agreeing to arbitration under these Rules the parties shall be taken to have agreed to apply only to the Tribunal, and not to any court of law or other judicial authority, for an order under Article 15.1, or for an order for security for costs under Article 15.2.

15.4 Without prejudice to the right of any party to apply to a competent court for pre-award conservatory measures (except those referred to in Articles 15.1 and 15.2), the Tribunal shall also have the power to order any party to provide security for all or part of any amount in dispute in the arbitration.

15.5 In the event that orders under paragraphs 1, 2, and 4 of this Article are not complied with, the Tribunal may disregard claims or counterclaims by the non-complying party, although it may proceed to determine claims or counterclaims by complying parties.

Article 16 The Award

16.1 The Tribunal shall make its award in writing and, unless all the parties agree otherwise, shall state the reasons upon which its award is based. The award shall state its date and shall be signed by the arbitrator or arbitrators.

16.2 If any arbitrator refuses or fails to comply with the mandatory provisions of any applicable law relating to the making of the award, having been given a reasonable opportunity to do so, the remaining arbitrators shall proceed in his absence.

16.3 Where there is more than one arbitrator and they fail to agree on any issue, they shall decide by a majority. Failing a majority decision on any issue, the Chairman of the Tribunal shall make the award alone as if he were sole arbitrator. If an arbitrator refuses or fails to sign the award, the signatures of the majority shall be sufficient, provided that the reason for the omitted signature is stated.

16.4 The sole arbitrator or chairman shall be responsible

for delivering the award to the Court, which shall transmit cerified copies to the parties provided that the costs of the arbitration have been paid to the Court in accordance with Article 18.

16.5 Awards may be expressed in any currency, and the Tribunal may award that simple or compound interest shall be paid by any party on any sum which is the subject of the reference at such rates as the Tribunal determines to be appropriate, without being bound by legal rates of interest, in respect of any period which the Tribunal determines to be appropriate ending not later than the date upon which the award is complied with.

16.6 The Tribunal may make separate final awards on different issues at different times, which shall be subject to correction under the procedure specified in Article 17. Such awards shall be enforceable.

16.7 In the event of a settlement, the Tribunal may render an award recording the settlement if any party so requests. If the parties do not require a consent award, then on confirmation in writing by the parties to the Court that a settlement has been reached the Tribunal shall be discharged and the reference to arbitration concluded, subject to payment by the parties of any outstanding costs of the arbitration in accordance with Article 18.

16.8 By agreeing to arbitration under these Rules, the parties undertake to carry out the award without delay, and waive their right to any form of appeal or recourse to a court of law or other judicial authority, insofar as such waiver may be validly made. Awards shall be final and binding on the parties as from the date they are made.

Article 17   Correction of Awards and Additional Awards

17.1 Within thirty days of receipt of the award, unless another period of time has been agreed upon by the parties, a party may by notice to the Registrar request the Tribunal to correct in the award any errors in computation, any clerical or typographical errors or any errors of a similar nature. If the Tribunal considers the request to be justified, it shall make the corrections within thirty days of receipt of the request. Any correction, which shall take the form of a separate memorandum, shall become part of the award.

17.2 The Tribunal may correct any error of the type referred to in Article 17.1 on its own initiative within thirty days of the date of the award.

17.3 Unless otherwise agreed by the parties, a party may, within thirty days of receipt of the award, and with notice to the other party or parties, request the Tribunal to make an additional award as to claims presented in the arbitral proceedings but not dealt with in the award. If the Tribunal considers the request to be justified, it shall make the additional award within sixty days.

17.4 The provisions of Article 16 shall apply mutatis mutandis to a correction of the award and to any additional award.

Article 18   Costs

18.1 The costs of the arbitration (other than the legal or other costs incurred by the parties themselves) shall be in accordance with the Schedule of Costs applicable to these Rules as of the date of the Request for Arbitration.

18.2 The Tribunal shall specify in the award the total amount of the costs of the arbitration, subject to the confirmation of the Court that the amount is in conformity with the Schedule of Costs. Unless the parties shall agree otherwise, the Tribunal shall determine the proportions in which the parties shall pay all or part of them to the Court. If the Tribunal has determined that all or any part of the costs of the arbitration shall be paid by any party other than a party which has already paid them to the Court, the latter shall have the right to recover the appropriate amount from the former.

18.3 The Tribunal shall have the authority to order in its award that all or a part of the legal or other costs of a party (apart from the costs of the arbitration) be paid by another party.

18.4 If the arbitration is abandoned, suspended or concluded, by agreement or otherwise, before the final award is made, the parties shall be jointly and severally liable to pay to the Court the costs of the arbitration as determined by the Tribunal, subject to the confirmation by the Court that the amount is in conformity with the Schedule of Costs. In the event that the costs so determined are less than the deposits made, there shall be a refund in such proportions as the parties may agree, or, failing agreement, in the same proportions as the deposits were made.

Article 19 Exclusion of Liability

19.1 Neither the court nor any arbitrator shall be liable to any party for any act or omission in connection with any arbitration conducted under these Rules, save that arbitrators (but not the Court) may be liable for the consequences of conscious and deliberate wrongdoing.

19.2 After the award has been made and the possibilities of correction and additional awards referred to in Article 17 have lapsed or been exhausted, neither the Court nor any arbitrator shall be under any obligation to make any statement to any person about any matter concerning the arbitration, nor shall any party seek to make any arbitrator or any officer of the Court a witness in any legal proceedings arising out of the arbitration.

Article 20 General Rules

20.1 A party who knows that any provision of, or requirement under, these Rules has not been compiled with and yet proceeds with the arbitration without promptly stating its objection to such non-compliance, shall be deemed to have waived its right to object.

20.2 In all matters not expressly provided for in these Rules, the Court and the Tribunal shall act in the spirit of these Rules and shall make every reasonable effort to ensure that the award is legally enforceable.

Schedule of Costs

(effective 1 January 1985)

Administrative Costs

(a) Up to and including initial appointment of the Tribunal by the Court (payable in advance with Request for arbitration) £200

(b) After initial appointment, for time spent by the Secretariat of the LCIA in the administration of the arbitration (payable with award or on interim invoice) £50 per hour

(c) Expenses incurred by the Secretariat of the LCIA in connection with the arbitration (payable with award or on interim invoice) at cost

(d) Additional arbitration support services, whether provided by the Secretariat of the LCIA from its own resources or otherwise (payable with award or on interim invoice) as appropriate

Costs of the Tribunal

(e) The Tribunal's fees will be calculated by reference to work done by its members in connection with the arbitration and will be charged at rates appropriate to the particular circumstances of the case, including its complexity and any special qualifications of the arbitrators. These rates will be advised by the Registrar of the Court to the parties at the time of the appointment of the Tribunal, but may be reviewed annually if the duration of the arbitration requires.

(By way of guidance, the rates for arbitrators fees on 1 January 1985 fell, in most cases, within the following range:

Time for meetings or hearings   £300–£1,250 per day

Other time spent on the arbitration   £60–£250 per hour

However, in exceptional cases the rates may be higher or lower.)

(f) Members of the Tribunal may charge at the full rate or such lesser rate as they consider appropriate for time spent travelling or time wasted by late postponement or cancellation.

(g) Where the Tribunal takes over the administration of the proceedings by arrangement with the Court, time spent by the Tribunal on administration thereafter will be charged at its hourly rate.

(h) Specific expenses incurred by the Tribunal in connection with the arbitration will be charged at cost.

(i) The Tribunal may require interim payments by the parties in respect of its costs, having regard to the duration or anticipated duration of the arbitration.

Notes

(a) Parties are jointly and severally liable to the LCIA for all costs of the arbitration until all such costs have been paid in full, but if any party pays any amount of such costs which the Tribunal directs should be paid by another party, the party paying shall be entitled to recover that amount from that other party.

(b) Value Added Tax may be added as appropriate.

(c) Fees will be invoiced in sterling but may be paid in other convertible currencies at rates prevailing at the time of payment.

(d) The rates quoted in this Schedule may be reviewed from time to time.

(e) Any dispute regarding administration costs or costs of the Tribunal shall be determined by the Court.

UNCITRAL Arbitration Rules (1976)

Scope of Application

Article 1. 1. Where the parties to a contract have agreed in writing* that disputes in relation to that contract shall be referred to arbitration under the UNCITRAL Arbitration Rules, then such disputes shall be settled in accordance with these Rules subject to such modifications as the parties may agree in writing.

2. These Rules shall govern the arbitration except that where any of these Rules is in conflict with a provision of the law applicable to the arbitration from which the parties cannot derogate, that provision shall prevail.

Notice, Calculation of Periods of Time

Article 2. 1. For the purposes of these Rules, any notice, including a notification, communication or proposal, is deemed to have been received if it is physically delivered to the addressee or if it is delivered at his habitual residence, place of business or mailing address, or, if none of these can be found after making reasonable inquiry, then at the addressee's last known residence or place of business. Notice shall be deemed to have been received on the day it is so delivered.

2. For the purposes of calculating a period of time under these Rules, such period shall begin to run on the day following the day when a notice, notification, communication or proposal is received. If the last day of such period is an official holiday or a non-business day at the residence or place of business of the addressee, the period is extended until the first business day which follows. Official holidays or non-business days occurring during the running of the period of time are included in calculating the period.

Notice of Arbitration

Article 3. 1. The party initiating recourse to arbitration (hereinafter called the 'claimant') shall give to the other party (hereinafter called the 'respondent') a notice of arbitration.

2. Arbitral proceedings shall be deemed to commence on the date on which the notice of arbitration is received by the respondent.

3. The notice of arbitration shall include the following:
(a) A demand that the dispute be referred to arbitration;
(b) The names and addresses of the parties;

---

* *Model Arbitration Clause*
Any dispute, controversy or claim arising out of or relating to this contract, or the breach, termination or invalidity thereof, shall be settled by arbitration in accordance with the UNCITRAL Arbitration Rules as at present in force.

Note – Parties may wish to consider adding:
(a) The appointing authority shall be . . . (name of institution or person);
(b) The number of arbitrators shall be . . . (one or three);
(c) The place of arbitration shall be . . . (town or country);
(d) The language(s) to be used in the arbitral proceedings shall be . . .

(c) A reference to the arbitration clause or the separate arbitration agreement that is invoked;

(d) A reference to the contract out of or in relation to which the dispute arises;

(e) The general nature of the claim and an indication of the amount involved, if any;

(f) The relief or remedy sought;

(g) A proposal as to the number of arbitrators (ie, one or three), if the parties have not previously agreed thereon.

4. The notice of arbitration may also include:

(a) The proposals for the appointments of a sole arbitrator and an appointing authority referred to in article 6, paragraph 1;

(b) The notification of the appointment of an arbitrator referred to in article 7;

(c) The statement of claim referred to in article 18.

Representation and Assistance

Article 4. The parties may be represented or assisted by persons of their choice. The names and addresses of such persons must be communicated in writing to the other party; such communication must specify whether the appointment is being made for purposes of representation or assistance.

SECTION II. COMPOSITION OF THE ARBITRAL TRIBUNAL

Number of Arbitrators

Article 5. If the parties have not previously agreed on the number of arbitrators (ie, one or three), and if within 15 days after the receipt by the respondent of the notice of arbitration the parties have not agreed that there shall be only one arbitrator, three arbitrators shall be appointed.

Appointment of Arbitrators (Articles 6 to 8)

Article 6. 1. If a sole arbitrator is to be appointed, either party may propose to the other:

(a) The names of one or more persons, one of whom would serve as the sole arbitrator; and

(b) If no appointing authority has been agreed upon by the parties, the name or names of one more institutions or persons, one of whom would serve as appointing authority.

2. If within 30 days after receipt by a party of a proposal made in accordance with paragraph 1 the parties have not reached agreement on the choice of a sole arbitrator, the sole arbitrator shall be appointed by the appointing authority agreed upon by the parties. If no appointing authority has been agreed upon by the parties, or if the appointing authority agreed upon refuses to act or fails to appoint the arbitrator within 60 days of the receipt of a party's request therefor, either party may request the Secretary-General of the Permanent Court of Arbitration at The Hague to designate an appointing authority.

3. The appointing authority shall, at the request of one of the parties, appoint the sole arbitrator as promptly as possible. In

making the appointment the appointing authority shall use the following list-procedure, unless both parties agree that the list-procedure should not be used or unless the appointing authority determines in its discretion that the use of the list-procedure is not appropriate for the case:

(a) At the request of one of the parties the appointing authority shall communicate to both parties an identical list containing at least three names;

(b) Within 15 days after the receipt of this list, each party may return the list to the appointing authority after having deleted the name or names to which he objects and numbered the remaining names on the list in the order of his preference;

(c) After the expiration of the above period of time the appointing authority shall appoint the sole arbitrator from among the names approved on the lists returned to it and in accordance with the order of preference indicated by the parties;

(d) If for any reason the appointment cannot be made according to this procedure, the appointing authority may exercise its discretion in appointing the sole arbitrator.

4. In making the appointment, the appointing authority shall have regard to such considerations as are likely to secure the appointment of an independent and impartial arbitrator and shall take into account as well the advisability of appointing an arbitrator of a nationality other than the nationalities of the parties.

Article 7. 1. If three arbitrators are to be appointed, each party shall appoint one arbitrator. The two arbitrators thus appointed shall choose the third arbitrator who will act as the presiding arbitrator of the tribunal.

2. If within 30 days after the receipt of a party's notification of the appointment of an arbitrator the other party has not notified the first party of the arbitrator he has appointed:

(a) The first party may request the appointing authority previously designated by the parties to appoint the second arbitrator; or

(b) If no such authority has been previously designated by the parties, or if the appointing authority previously designated refuses to act or fails to appoint the arbitrator within 30 days after receipt of a party's request therefor, the first party may request the Secretary-General of the Permanent Court of Arbitration at The Hague to designate the appointing authority. The first party may then request the appointing authority so designated to appoint the second arbitrator. In either case, the appointing authority may exercise its discretion in appointing the arbitrator.

3. If within 30 days after the appointment of the second arbitrator the two arbitrators have not agreed on the choice of the presiding arbitrator, the presiding arbitrator shall be appointed by an appointing authority in the same way as a sole arbitrator would be appointed under article 6.

Article 8. 1. When an appointing authority is requested to appoint an arbitrator pursuant to article 6 or article 7, the party which makes the request shall send to the appointing authority a copy of the notice of arbitration, a copy of the contract out of or in relation to which the dispute has arisen and a copy of the arbitration agreement if it is not contained in the contract. The appointing authority may require from either party such information as it deems necessary to fulfil its function.

2. Where the names of one or more persons are proposed for appointments as arbitrators, their full names, addresses and nationalities shall be indicated, together with a description of their qualifications.

Challenge of Arbitrators (Articles 9 to 12)

Article 9. A prospective arbitrator shall disclose to those who approach him in connexion with his possible appointment any circumstances likely to give rise to justifiable doubts as to his impartiality or independence. An arbitrator, once appointed or chosen, shall disclose such circumstances to the parties unless they have already been informed by him of these circumstances.

Article 10. 1. Any arbitrator may be challenged if circumstances exist that give rise to justifiable doubts as to the arbitrator's impartiality or independence.

2. A party may challenge the arbitrator appointed by him only for reasons of which he becomes aware after the appointment has been made.

Article 11. 1. A party who intends to challenge an arbitrator shall send notice of his challenge within 15 days after the appointment of the challenged arbitrator has been notified to the challenging party or within 15 days after the circumstances mentioned in articles 9 and 10 became known to that party.

2. The challenge shall be notified to the other party, to the arbitrator who is challenged and to the other members of the arbitral tribunal. The notification shall be in writing and shall state the reasons for the challenge.

3. When an arbitrator has been challenged by one party, the other party may agree to the challenge. The arbitrator may also, after the challenge, withdraw from his office. In neither case does this imply acceptance of the validity of the grounds for the challenge. In both cases the procedure provided in article 6 or 7 shall be used in full for the appointment of the substitute arbitrator, even if during the process of appointing the challenged arbitrator a party had failed to exercise his right to appoint or to participate in the appointment.

Article 12. 1. If the other party does not agree to the challenge and the challenged arbitrator does not withdraw, the decision on the challenge will be made:

(a) When the initial appointment was made by an appointing authority, by that authority;

(b) When the initial appointment was not made by an appointing authority, but an appointing authority has been previously designated, by that authority;

(c) In all other cases, by the appointing authority to be designated in accordance with the procedure for designating an appointing authority as provided for in article 6.

2. If the appointing authority sustains the challenge, a substitute arbitrator shall be appointed or chosen pursuant to the procedure applicable to the appointment or choice of an arbitrator as provided in articles 6 to 9 except that, when this procedure would call for the designation of an appointing authority, the appointment of the arbitrator shall be made by the appointing authority which decided on the challenge.

Replacement of an Arbitrator

Article 13. 1. In the event of the death or resignation of an arbitrator during the course of the arbitral proceedings, a substitute arbitrator shall be appointed or chosen pursuant to the procedure provided for in articles 6 to 9 that was applicable to the appointment or choice of the arbitrator being replaced.

2. In the event that an arbitrator fails to act or in the event of the *de jure* or *de facto* impossibility of his performing his functions, the procedure in respect of the challenge and replacement of an arbitrator as provided in the preceding articles shall apply.

Repetition of Hearings in the Event of the Replacement of an Arbitrator

Article 14. If under articles 11 to 13 the sole or presiding arbitrator is replaced, any hearings held previously shall be repeated; if any other arbitrator is replaced, such prior hearings may be repeated at the discretion of the arbitral tribunal.

SECTION III: ARBITRAL PROCEEDINGS

General Provisions

Article 15. Subject to these Rules, the arbitral tribunal may conduct the arbitration in such manner as it considers appropriate, provided that the parties are treated with equality and that at any stage of the proceedings each party is given a full opportunity of presenting his case.

2. If either party so requests at any stage of the proceedings, the arbitral tribunal shall hold hearings for the presentation of evidence by witnesses, including expert witnesses, or for oral argument. In the absence of such a request, the arbitral tribunal shall decide whether to hold such hearings or whether the proceedings shall be conducted on the basis of documents and other materials.

3. All documents or information supplied to the arbitral tribunal by one party shall at the same time be communicated by that party to the other party.

Place of Arbitration

Article 16. 1. Unless the parties have agreed upon the place where the arbitration is to be held, such places shall be determined by the arbitral tribunal, having regard to the circumstances of the arbitration.

2. The arbitral tribunal may determine the locale of the arbitration within the country agreed upon by the parties. It may hear witnesses and hold meetings for consultation among its members at any place it deems appropriate, having regard to the circumstances of the arbitration.

3. The arbitral tribunal may meet at any place it deems appropriate for the inspection of goods, other property or documents. The parties shall be given sufficient notice to enable them to be present at such inspection.

4. The award shall be made at the place of arbitration.

Language

Article 17. 1. Subject to an agreement by the parties, the arbitral tribunal shall, promptly after its appointment, determine the language or languages to be used in the proceedings. This determination shall apply to the statement of claim, the statement of defence, and any further written statements and, if oral hearings take place, to the language or languages to be used in such hearings.

2. The arbitral tribunal may order that any documents annexed to the statement of claim or statement of defence, and any supplementary documents or exhibits submitted in the course of the proceedings, delivered in their original language, shall be accompanied by a translation into the language or languages agreed upon by the parties or determined by the arbitral tribunal.

Statement of Claim

Article 18. 1. Unless the statement of claim was contained in the notice of arbitration, within a period of time to be determined by the arbitral tribunal, the claimant shall communicate his statement of claim in writing to the respondent and to each of the arbitrators. A copy of the contract, and of the arbitration agreement if not contained in the contract, shall be annexed thereto.

2. The statement of claim shall include the following particulars:
(a) The names and addresses of the parties;
(b) A statement of the facts supporting the claim;
(c) The points at issue;
(d) The relief or remedy sought.
The claimant may annex to his statement of claim all documents he deems relevant or may add a reference to the documents or other evidence he will submit.

Statement of Defence

Article 19. 1. Within a period of time to be determined by the arbitral tribunal, the respondent shall communicate his statement of defence in writing to the claimant and to each of the arbitrators.

2. The statement of defence shall reply to the particulars (b), (c) and (d) of the statement of claim (article 18, paragraph 2). The respondent may annex to his statement the documents on which he relies for his defence or may add a reference to the documents or other evidence he will submit.

3. In his statement of defence, or at a later stage in the arbitral proceedings if the arbitral tribunal decides that the delay was justified under the circumstances, the respondent may make a counter-claim arising out of the same contract or rely on a claim arising out of the same contract for the purpose of a set-off.

4. The provisions of article 18, paragraph 2, shall apply to a counter-claim and a claim relied on for the purpose of a set-off.

Amendments to the Claim or Defence

Article 20. During the course of the arbitral proceedings either party may amend or supplement his claim or defence unless the arbitral tribunal considers it inappropriate to allow such amendment having regard to the delay in making it or prejudice to the other party or any other circumstances. However, a claim may not be amended in such a manner that the amended claim falls outside the scope of the arbitration clause or separate arbitration agreement.

Pleas as to the Jurisdiction of the Arbitral Tribunal

Article 21. 1. The arbitral tribunal shall have the power to rule on objections that it has no jurisdiction, including any objections with respect to the existence or validity of the arbitration clause or of the separate arbitration agreement.

2. The arbitral tribunal shall have the power to determine the existence or the validity of the contract of which an arbitration clause forms a part. For the purposes of article 21, an arbitration clause which forms part of a contract and which provides for arbitration under these Rules shall be treated as an agreement independent of the other terms of the contract. A decision by the arbitral tribunal that the contract is null and void shall not entail *ipso jure* the invalidity of the arbitration clause.

3. A plea that the arbitral tribunal does not have jurisdiction shall be raised not later than in the statement of defence or, with respect to a counter-claim, in the reply to the counter-claim.

4. In general, the arbitral tribunal should rule on a plea concerning its jurisdiction as a preliminary question. However, the arbitral tribunal may proceed with the arbitration and rule on such a plea in their final award.

Further Written Statements

Article 22. The arbitral tribunal shall decide which further written statements, in addition to the statement of claim and the statement of defence, shall be required from the parties or may be presented by them and shall fix the periods of time for communicating such statements.

Periods of Time

Article 23. The periods of time fixed by the arbitral tribunal for the communication of written statements (including the statement of claim and statement of defence) should not exceed 45 days. However, the arbitral tribunal may extend the time-limits if it concludes that an extension is justified.

Evidence and Hearings (Articles 24 and 25)

Article 24. 1. Each party shall have the burden of proving the facts relied on to support his claim or defence.

2. The arbitral tribunal may, if it considers it appropriate, require a party to deliver to the tribunal and to the other party, within such a period of time as the arbitral tribunal shall decide, a summary of the documents and other evidence which that party intends to present in support of the facts in issue set out in his statement of claim or statement of defence.

3. At any time during the arbitral proceedings the arbitral tribunal may require the parties to produce documents, exhibits or other evidence within such a period of time as the tribunal shall determine.

Article 25. 1. In the event of an oral hearing, the arbitral tribunal shall give the parties adequate advance notice of the date, time and place thereof.

2. If witnesses are to be heard, at least 15 days before the hearing each party shall communicate to the arbitral tribunal and to the other party the names and addresses of the witnesses he intends to present, the subject upon and the languages in which such witnesses will give their testimony.

3. The arbitral tribunal shall make arrangements for the translation of oral statements made at a hearing and for a record of the hearing if either is deemed necessary by the tribunal under the circumstances of the case, or if the parties have agreed thereto and have communicated such agreement to the tribunal at least 15 days before the hearing.

4. Hearings shall be held *in camera* unless the parties agree otherwise. The arbitral tribunal may require the retirement of any witness or witnesses during the testimony of other witnesses. The arbitral tribunal is free to determine the manner in which witnesses are examined.

5. Evidence of witnesses may also be presented in the form of written statements signed by them.

6. The arbitral tribunal shall determine the admissibility, relevance, materiality and weight of the evidence offered.

Interim Measures of Protection

Article 26. 1. At the request of either party, the arbitral tribunal may take any interim measures it deems necessary in respect of the subject-matter of the dispute, including measures for the conservation of the goods forming the subject-matter in dispute, such as ordering their deposit with a third person or the sale of perishable goods.

2. Such interim measures may be established in the form of an interim award. The arbitral tribunal shall be entitled to require security for the costs of such measures.

3. A request for interim measures addressed by any party to a judicial authority shall not be deemed incompatible with the agreement to arbitrate, or as a waiver of that agreement.

Experts

Article 27. 1. The arbitral tribunal may appoint one or more experts to report to it, in writing, on specific issues to be determined by the tribunal. A copy of the expert's terms of reference, established by the arbitral tribunal, shall be communicated to the parties.

2. The parties shall give the expert any relevant information or produce for his inspection any relevant documents or goods that he may require of them. Any dispute between a party and such expert as to the relevance of the required information or production shall be referred to the arbitral tribunal for decision.

3. Upon receipt of the expert's report, the arbitral tribunal shall communicate a copy of the report to the parties who shall be given the opportunity to express, in writing, their opinion on the report. A party shall be entitled to examine any document on which the expert has relied in his report.

4. At the request of either party the expert, after delivery of the report, may be heard at a hearing where the parties shall have the opportunity to be present and to interrogate the expert. At this hearing either party may present expert witnesses in order to testify on the points at issue. The provisions of article 25 shall be applicable to such proceedings.

Default

Article 28. 1. If, within the period of time fixed by the arbitral tribunal, the claimant has failed to communicate his claim without showing sufficient cause for such failure, the arbitral tribunal shall issue an order for the termination of the arbitral proceedings. If, within the period of time fixed by the arbitral tribunal, the respondent has failed to communicate his statement of defence without showing sufficient cause for such failure, the arbitral tribunal shall order that the proceedings continue.

2. If one of the parties, duly notified under these Rules, fails to appear at a hearing, without showing sufficient cause for such failure, the arbitral tribunal may proceed with the arbitration.

3. If one of the parties, duly invited to produce documentary evidence fails to so so within the established period of time, without showing sufficient cause for such failure, the arbitral tribunal may make the award on the evidence before it.

Closure of Hearings

Article 29. 1. The arbitral tribunal may inquire of the parties if they have any further proof to offer or witnesses to be heard or submissions to make and, if there are none, it may declare the hearing closed.

2. The arbitral tribunal may, if it considers it necessary owing to exceptional circumstances, decide, on its own motion or upon application of a party, to reopen the hearings at any time before the award is made.

Waiver Rules

Article 30. A party who knows that any provision of, or requirement under, these Rules have not been complied with and yet proceeds with the arbitration without promptly stating his objection to such non-compliance, shall be deemed to have waived his right to object.

SECTION IV. THE AWARD

Decisions

Article 31. 1. When there are three arbitrators, any award or other decisions of the arbitral tribunal shall be made by a majority of the arbitrators.

2. In the case of questions of procedure, when there is no majority or when the arbitral tribunal so authorizes, the presiding arbitrator may decide on his own, subject to revision, if any, by the arbitral tribunal.

Form and Effect of the Award

Article 32. 1. In addition to making a final award, the arbitral tribunal shall be entitled to make interim, interlocutory, or partial awards.

2. The award shall be made in writing and shall be final and binding on the parties. The parties undertake to carry out the award without delay.

3. The arbitral tribunal shall state the reasons upon which the award is based, unless the parties have agreed that no reasons are to be given.

4. An award shall be signed by the arbitrators and it shall contain the date on which and the place where the award was made. Where there are three arbitrators and one of them fails to sign, the award shall state the reason for the absence of the signature.

5. The award may be made public only with the consent of both parties.

6. Copies of the award signed by the arbitrators shall be communicated to the parties by the arbitral tribunal.

7. If the arbitration law of the country where the award is made requires that the award be filed or registered by the arbitral tribunal, the tribunal shall comply with this requirement within the period of time required by law.

Applicable Law, Amiable Compositeur

Article 33. 1. The arbitral tribunal shall apply the law designated by the parties as applicable to the substance of the dispute. Failing such designation by the parties, the arbitral tribunal shall apply the law determined by the conflict of laws rules which it considers applicable.

2. The arbitral tribunal shall decide as *amiable compositeur* or *ex aequo et bono* only if the parties have expressly authorized the arbitral tribunal to do so and if the law applicable to the arbitral procedure permits such arbitration.

3. In all cases, the arbitral tribunal shall decide in accordance with the terms of the contract and shall take into account the usages of the trade applicable to the transaction.

Settlement or Other Grounds for Termination

Article 34. 1. If, before the award is made, the parties agree on a settlement of the dispute, the arbitral tribunal shall either issue an order for the termination of the arbitral proceedings or, if requested by both parties and accepted by the tribunal, record the settlement in the form of an arbitral award on agreed terms. The arbitral tribunal is not obliged to give reasons for such an award.

2. If, before the award is made, the continuation of the arbitral proceedings becomes unnecessary or impossible for any reason not mentioned in paragraph 1, the arbitral tribunal shall inform the parties of its intention to issue an order for the termination of the proceedings. The arbitral tribunal shall have the power to issue such an order unless a party raises justifiable grounds for objection.

3. Copies of the order for termination of the arbitral proceedings or of the arbitral award on agreed terms, signed by the arbitrators, shall be communicated by the arbitral tribunal to the parties. Where an arbitral award on agreed terms is made, the provisions of article 32, paragraphs 2 and 4 to 7, shall apply.

Interpretation of the Award

Article 35. 1. Within 30 days after the receipt of the award, either party, with notice to the other party, may request that the arbitral tribunal give an interpretation of the award.

2. The interpretation shall be given in writing within 45 days after the receipt of the request. The interpretation shall form part of the award and the provisions of article 32, paragraphs 2 to 7, shall apply.

Correction of the Award

Article 36. 1. Within 30 days after the receipt of the award, either party, with notice to the other party, may request the arbitral tribunal to correct in the award any errors in computation, any clerical or typographical errors, or any errors of similar nature. The arbitral tribunal may within 30 days after the communication of the award make such corrections on its own initiative.

2. Such corrections shall be in writing, and the provisions of article 32, paragraphs 2 to 7, shall apply.

Additional Award

Article 37. 1. Within 30 days after the receipt of the award, either party, with notice to the other party, may request the arbitral tribunal to make an additional award as to claims presented in the arbitral proceedings but omitted from the award.

2. If the arbitral tribunal considers the request for an additional award to be justified and considers that the omission can be rectified without any further hearings or evidence, it shall complete its award within 60 days after the receipt of the request.

3. When an additional awards is made, the provisions of article 32, paragraphs 2 to 7, shall apply.

Costs (Articles 38 to 40)

Article 38. The arbitral tribunal shall fix the costs of arbitration in its award. The term 'costs' includes only:

(a) The fees of the arbitral tribunal to be stated separately as to each arbitrator and to be fixed by the tribunal itself in accordance with article 39;

(b) The travel and other expenses incurred by the arbitrators;

(c) The costs of expert advice and of other assistance required by the arbitral tribunal;

(d) The travel and other expenses of witnesses to the extent such expenses are approved by the arbitral tribunal;

(e) The costs for legal representation and assistance of the successful party if such costs were claimed during the arbitral proceedings, and only to the extent that the arbitral tribunal determines that the amount of such costs is reasonable;

(f) Any fees and expenses of the appointing authority as well as the expenses of the Secretary-General of the Permanent Court of Arbitration at The Hague.

Article 39. 1. The fees of the arbitral tribunal shall be reasonable in amount, taking into account the amount in dispute, the complexity of the subject-matter, the time spent by the arbitrators and any other relevant circumstances of the case.

2. If an appointing authority has been agreed upon by the parties or designated by the Secretary-General of the Permanent Court of Arbitration at The Hague, and if that authority has issued a schedule of fees for arbitrators in international cases which it administers, the arbitral tribunal in fixing its fees shall take that schedule of fees into account to the extent that it considers appropriate in the circumstances of the case.

3. If such appointing authority has not issued a schedule of fees for arbitrators in international cases, any party may at any time request the appointing authority to furnish a statement setting forth the basis for establishing fees which is customarily followed in international cases in which the authority appoints arbitrators. If the appointing authority consents to provide such a statement, the arbitral tribunal in fixing its fees shall take such information into account to the extent that it considers appropriate in the circumstances of the case.

4. In cases referred to in paragraphs 2 and 3, when a party so requests and the appointing authority consents to perform the function, the arbitral tribunal shall fix its fees only after consultation with the appointing authority which may make any comment it deems appropriate to the arbitral tribunal concerning the fees.

Article 40 1. Except as provided in paragraph 2, the costs of arbitration shall in principle be borne by the unsuccessful party. However, the arbitral tribunal may apportion each of such costs between the parties if it determines that apportionment is reasonable, taking into account the circumstances of the case.

2. With respect to the costs of legal representation and assistance referred to in article 38, paragraph (e), the arbitral tribunal, taking into account the circumstances of the case, shall be free to determine which party shall bear such costs or may apportion such costs between the parties if it determines that apportionment is reasonable.

3. When the arbitral tribunal issues an order for the termination of the arbitral proceedings or makes an award on agreed terms, it shall fix the costs of arbitration referred to in article 38 and article 39, paragraph 1, in the text of that order or award.

4. No additional fees may be charged by an arbitral tribunal for interpretation or correction or completion of its award under articles 35 to 37.

Deposit of Costs

Article 41. 1. The arbitral tribunal, on its establishment, may request each party to deposit an equal amount as an advance for the costs referred to in article 38, paragraphs (a), (b) and (c).

2. During the course of the arbitral proceedings the arbitral tribunal may request supplementary deposits from the parties.

3. If an appointing authority has been agreed upon by the parties or designated by the Secretary-General of the Permanent Court of Arbitration at The Hague, and when a party so requests and the appointing authority consents to perform the function, the arbitral tribunal shall fix the amounts of any deposits or supplementary deposits only after consultation with the appointing authority which may make any comments to the arbitral tribunal which it deems appropriate concerning the amount of such deposits and supplementary deposits.

4. If the required deposits are not paid in full within 30 days after the receipt of the request, the arbitral tribunal shall so inform the parties in order that one or another of them may make the required payment. If such payment is not made, the arbitral tribunal may order the suspension or termination of the arbitral proceedings.

5. After the award has been made, the arbitral tribunal shall render an accounting to the parties of the deposits received and return any unexpended balance to the parties.

International Bar Association Supplementary Rules on Evidence in International Commercial Arbitration (1983)

International arbitration in its various aspects has engaged the attention of several expert and specialist bodies, including the International Bar Association. The section on Business Law of the IBA produced in May 1983 a set of 'Supplementary Rules Governing the Presentation and Reception of Evidence in International Commercial Arbitration'.

These Rules are solely concerned with the presentation and reception of evidence in arbitrations and are recommended by the International Bar Association for incorporation in, or adoption together with, institutional and other general rules or procedures governing international commercial arbitrations.

Even if not specifically adopted by agreement between the parties, they can serve as a guide to arbitrators conducting such arbitrations when the parties in contention come from law areas having rules of procedures derived from different systems.

It is recommended by the I.B.A. that when the parties desire to adopt the I.B.A. Rules of Evidence as supplementary to the general rules applicable to a particular arbitration, the following additional clause be adopted:

'The I.B.A. Rules of Evidence shall apply together with the General Rules governing any submission to arbitration incorporated in this Contract. Where they are inconsistent with the aforesaid General Rules, these I.B.A. Rules of Evidence shall prevail but solely as regards the presentation and reception of evidence.'

The IBA Rules of Evidence Supplementary rules governing the presentation and reception of evidence in international commercial arbitration

Article 1
Scope of Application

1 These are procedural rules governing the presentation of evidence ('the Rules of Evidence') intended to supplement any other rules applicable to the arbitration ('the General Rules'). If the parties have so agreed in writing the Rules of Evidence shall govern the arbitration if and so far as they are not in conflict with mandatory applicable provisions of law. The parties may at any time agree in writing to amend, add to or delete any provision contained in the Rules of Evidence.

2 In so far as the Rules of Evidence and the General Rules applicable to the arbitration are silent, the Arbitrator may in his discretion conduct the taking of evidence as he thinks fit.

3 In case of conflict between any provisions of the Rules of Evidence and the General Rules, the Rules of Evidence shall prevail unless the parties shall otherwise agree in writing.

Article 2
Definitions

'*Arbitrator*' means a single arbitrator, or the panel of arbitrators or a majority of them as the case may be and shall include an umpire;

'*Claimant*' means the party or parties who commenced the arbitration or made the first claim therein;

'*Defendant*' means the party or parties against whom the Claimant made his claim and includes a party making a counter-claim;

'*General Rules*' means the specific rules of arbitration agreed upon by the parties except in so far as evidence is concerned;

'*Introductory Submissions*' means any Request for Arbitration or Statement of Claim or similar document produced by the Claimant, any Answer or Statement of Defence or similar document produced by the Defendant and any other or further documents in the nature of pleadings or submissions, however they may be denominated, produced by the parties in accordance with the General Rules, as well as any further submissions which the General Rules may require to be made before the hearings;

'*Production of Documents*' means the listing of documents relevant to the subject matter of the claims and defences in issue in the possession, custody, or control of a party and the delivery of the List and of copies of such documents to the other parties to the arbitration and to the Arbitrator in accordance with the provisions of these Rules;

'*Witness Statement*' means a written statement complying with the provisions of Article 5 (2) below.

Article 3
Introductory
Submissions

The Introductory Submissions made by any party shall contain (*inter alia*) the means by which the facts relevant to the dispute are intended to be proved by that party, including, for each of such facts, the names of witnesses and reference to documents.

Article 4
Production of
Documents

1 Each party shall make Production of Documents in respect of all documentation on which such party desires to rely.

2 No later than sixty days after delivery of the last Introductory Submission made by the Defendant or by the date agreed between the parties or determined by the Arbitrator, each party shall exchange his List with every other party and deliver his List to the Arbitrator. Unless a document has been so listed it shall not be produced at the hearing without the consent of the Arbitrator. All documents in the List shall be numbered consecutively,

and shall be produced in their entirety unless otherwise agreed or ordered. Each party shall provide the Arbitrator with a copy of each document in his List.

3 A party shall at any time be entitled to a copy of any document listed by another party upon offer of payment of the reasonable copying charge. Such document shall be supplied within fifteen days of the request.

4 A party may by Notice to Produce a Document request any other party to provide him with any document relevant to the dispute between the parties and not listed, provided such document is identified with reasonable particularity and provided further that it passed to or from such other party from or to a third party who is not a party to the arbitration. If a party refuses to comply with a Notice to Produce a Document he may be ordered to do so by the Arbitrator.

5 The Arbitrator shall have the power, upon application by one of the parties or of his own volition, to order a party to produce any relevant document within such party's possession, custody or control.

6 If a party fails to comply with the Arbitrator's order to produce any relevant document within such party's possession, custody or control, the Arbitrator shall draw his conclusions from such failure.

Article 5
Witnesses

1 Within sixty days of the delivery of the last Introductory Submission made by the Defendant or by the date agreed between the parties or determined by the Arbitrator, all parties shall deliver their Witness Statements to the Arbitrator only.

2 Each Witness Statement shall:

(a) contain the full names and address of the Witness, his relationship to or connection with any of the parties, and a description of his background, qualifications, training and experience if these are relevant to the dispute or to the contents of his Statement;

(b) contain a full statement of the evidence it is desired by that party to present through the testimony of that witness;

(c) reflect whether the witness is a witness of fact or an expert, and whether the witness is testifying from his own knowledge, observation or experience, or from information and belief, and if the latter, the source of his knowledge; and

(d) be signed by the witness, and give the date and place of signature.

3 When the Arbitrator has received the Witness Statement(s) of each party he shall simultaneously deliver copies of all the Witness Statement(s) to all the other parties to the arbitration.

4 Within forty days of the receipt of any Witness Statement from another party a party may submit further or supplementary Witness Statements or Oral Evidence Notices in response to evidence submitted by such other party.

5 Within twenty days of the receipt of any Witness Statement any party may by notice to the Arbitrator and all other parties (an 'Oral Evidence Notice') request the right himself to give oral evidence at the hearing, or for any of his own witnesses or the witnesses of any other party to give oral evidence at the hearing. An Oral Evidence Notice shall stipulate the issues to which that evidence is to relate.

6 Within twenty days of the receipt of any Oral Evidence Notice all parties shall reply thereto. If a party fails to reply he shall be deemed to have agreed to the request contained in that Oral Evidence Notice. If all parties agree, or are deemed to have agreed, to a particular Oral Evidence Notice, the witness named therein shall give oral evidence at the hearing in accordance with the Oral Evidence Notice. The Arbitrator may himself order that any witness gives oral evidence.

7 If a party objects to an Oral Evidence Notice he shall state his reasons, and the question whether the witness shall give oral evidence and, if so, the issues upon which the evidence shall be given, shall be determined by the Arbitrator in his discretion. The Arbitrator may give his

decision on this question on the basis of the documents submitted or after hearing the parties, as he may decide.

8 A party may be heard in support of his own case. It shall be proper for a party or his legal advisers to interview witnesses or potential witnesses.

9 Any witness who gives oral evidence shall in the first place by questioned by the Arbitrator, and thereafter submit to examination by the party calling him, cross-examination by all other parties and re-examination by the party calling him.

10 The Arbitrator shall at all times have complete control over the procedure in relation to a witness giving oral evidence, including the right to limit or deny the right of a party to examine, cross-examine or re-examine a witness when it appears to the Arbitrator that such evidence or examination is unlikely to serve any further relevant purpose.

11 The testimony of any witness not giving oral evidence or of a witness in respect of any portion of his evidence not subject to oral testimony, shall be taken by means of his Witness Statement only.

12 A party shall be entitled to stipulate the name of a witness in his Oral Evidence Notice even if no Witness Statement has been produced for that witness, provided that the party states in writing that he has requested the witness to give a Witness Statement but that the witness has refused to do so and that the party has no power to compel him to provide such Statement. If the witness has given the party an informal or partial statement or other document (whether signed or not) the party shall deliver a copy thereof to the Arbitrator and to the other parties at the time he delivers the Oral Evidence Notice relating to that witness.

13 The Arbitrator shall decide what weight to attach to the evidence or Statements of any witness or party.

14 Nothing herein shall preclude the Arbitrator in his discretion from permitting any witness to give oral or written evidence.

Article 6
Scope of proceedings

1 Whenever Terms of Reference or the like are provided for in the General Rules or the parties so agree or the Abitrator so directs, a list of those witnesses shall be included who will be called to give oral evidence at the hearing and the issues upon which each witness will testify.

2 The Arbitrator may provide for such other matters concerning evidence as he considers advisable with a view to facilitating the conduct of the arbitration.

Article 7
Arbitrator's Powers

In addition to the powers available to him under the applicable procedural law and the General Rules under which the arbitration is conducted, the Arbitrator shall have the following powers:

(a) to vary, extend or limit any time-periods provided in the Rules of Evidence, or previously ordered by him:

(b) to order that a witness whose Witness Statement has been delivered be available to be called by any party;

(c) to call witnesses to testify orally or in writing, whether the parties agree thereto or not;

(d) to rule that a witness' evidence be ignored if the witness fails to appear without good cause;

(e) to rely on his own expert knowledge;

(f) to appoint experts to assist him or to give expert evidence or reports in the arbitration;

(g) to regulate the right of the parties to call expert witnesses and to make provisions with regard to their activities and the presentation of their evidence; and

(h) to exercise all the powers he deems necessary to make the arbitration effective and its conduct efficient as regards the taking of evidence.

28 May 1983

Part Three · *Precedents*

Note: The precedents set out in this part of the book relate to an international case (see Chapter 6, page 35) conducted under the 1978 edition of the rules of the London Court of Arbitration (as the London Court of International Arbitration was then called), but are fully illustrative of domestic and international cases conducted under the rules of the Chartered Institute of Arbitrators and the London Court.

The agreement

On 9th January 1980 an agreement was executed between CD Ltd (the Respondent in the arbitration which followed) and Mr Z (the Claimant) in the following form:

AGREEMENT

CD LIMITED with registered office at London and with operating office at Hampshire England of the one part and

MR Z of France of the other part

HEREBY AGREE AS FOLLOWS

1. CD hereby engages Z who hereby accepts for a period commencing on the first day of September nineteen hundred and seventy nine and ending on the thirty first day of August nineteen hundred and eighty one as an independent consultant to assist CD in widening the areas where its influence could be extended and in improving its ability to bid for complete turnkey projects ('projects').

2. In particular the duties of Z will include the following:
   (a) The publicising of CD and promoting its potential to undertake projects in the engineering field with persons and concerns in Continental Europe and other areas to be agreed;
   (b) The providing of a good liaison with customers after contracts relating to projects have been entered into;

(c) The assisting of CD in the obtaining of payment under such contracts.

3. Z's duties will be performed wholly outside the United Kingdom. Z may however from time to time be asked to visit the operating offices of CD to receive instructions. In this event clause 5 below will apply.

4. In consideration of the services to be rendered by Z under this Agreement CD will pay to Z as inclusive remuneration an annual fee of £   payable in quarterly instalments in advance upon receipt of Z's invoice and in the manner prescribed in such invoice.

5. If Z or any of his staff are required by CD to travel away from the Geneva area or to entertain CD will in addition to the payment referred to in clause 4 above reimburse the expenses incurred by reason of such travel or entertainment against production of vouchers receipts etc. provided always that such travel and entertaining have been authorised in writing before being undertaken by the Managing Director of CD.

6. Either party to this Agreement shall have the right to terminate it by notice to the other if that other of them shall breach either expressly or impliedly any of the obligations on its part to be observed or performed under this Agreement and shall fail to remedy such breach within 15 days of notice to it requiring such breach to be remedied. The notice to terminate shall take effect upon the thirtieth day after it was given in accordance with clause 8 below.

7. In the event of this Agreement being terminated because of Z's breach thereof but only for this reason Z will cease as from the final date of termination to be entitled to any further payments under clause 4 above but will remain entitled to payments already received under that clause and to the reimbursement under clause 5 above of expenses incurred in relation to travel or entertainment authorised prior to such date.

8. Any notice consent or other communication authorised or required to be given under this Agreement or for the purposes thereof shall be deemed to be sufficiently given to either party if sent by registered mail or recorded delivery service telex or telegraph addressed to such party at the address hereinbefore written and every notice consent or other

communication shall be deemed to have been received and given at the time when in the ordinary course of transmission it should have been delivered at the address to which it was sent.

9. Z undertakes not to use or to disclose to third parties any information which he may acquire as a result of this Agreement other than is strictly necessary for the fulfilment of his obligations hereunder.

10. Any amendment to this Agreement shall be in writing and shall be signed for and on behalf of the parties and shall enter into effect as provided for by the amendment.

11. The words 'in writing' or 'written' whenever contained in this Agreement shall be deemed to include any communication sent by one party to the other by letter telegraph or telex.

12. The validity construction and performance of this Agreement shall be governed by the law of England.

13. Any and all disputes arising out of or in connection with this Agreement including its validity construction and performance shall be determined by a sole arbitrator appointed under the rules of the London Court of Arbitration.

For and on behalf of
CD Limited

....
          Director   Z

Date: Date:

Note: Under this agreement (i) the proper law of the agreement (see Chapter 3, page 12) was declared by clause 12 to be the law of England; and (ii) by clause 13 all disputes (see Chapter 3, pages 11, 12) were to be determined by a sole arbitrator appointed under the Rules of the London Court of Arbitration (as the London Court of International Arbitration was then called – see Chapter 3, page 18).

The reference

The agreement was terminated later in 1980 and the parties applied to the London Court for appointment of a sole arbitrator as provided by clause 13 of the agreement. The Court made the appointment and under the rules the pleadings, i.e. the statement of case on behalf of the claimant and the statement of defence by the respondent, were delivered to the other party, to the Court and to the arbitrator.

This was a case in which the arbitration was 'administered' by the Court (see Chapter 4, page 21). Accordingly the first step taken by the Court was the appointment of the arbitrator in the form following.

IN THE MATTER OF THE ARBITRATION ACTS 1950 to 1979

AND

IN THE MATTER OF AN ARBITRATION UNDER THE RULES OF THE LONDON COURT OF ARBITRATION (1978 Edition)

BETWEEN   Z   <u>Claimant</u>

AND   CD Limited   <u>Respondent</u>

APPOINTMENT OF ARBITRATOR

WHEREAS:

(1) The Claimant and the Respondent are parties to an Agreement in writing made between them and dated 9th January 1980 which agreement contains the following arbitration clause:

'13. Any and all disputes arising out of or in connection with this Agreement including its validity construction and performance shall be determined by a sole arbitrator appointed under the rules of the London Court of Arbitration.'

AND WHEREAS:

(2)　Such a dispute as above has arisen between the parties

(3)　A Request for Arbitration has been made by the Claimant to the London Court of Arbitration ('the Court') which request has been duly accepted by the Court under its 1978 Rules being the rules current at the date of the said Agreement and in force at the date hereof

NOW THEREFORE I　　　　　　, President of the Chartered Institute of Arbitrators, and acting on behalf of the Court, DO HEREBY APPOINT as Sole Arbitrator herein:

>J F Phillips Esq CBE LLM FCIArb Barrister
>1 Verulam Buildings
>Gray's Inn, LONDON WC1

GIVEN UNDER MY HAND this 24th day of November 1980 at the London Court of Arbitration, 75 Cannon Street, London EC4

(signed) ....
For London Court of Arbitration

I, John Phillips of 1 Verulam Buildings, Gray's Inn, London WC1, Barrister, DO HEREBY ACCEPT the above mentioned appointment and request the Registrar to send forthwith to each of the parties or their representatives a copy of this Appointment and Acceptance.

(Signed) ....
Sole Arbitrator

Dated:

Note: Where the case is not to be administered by the Court or any other organisation, but by the arbitrator himself, the first step after acceptance of appointment by the arbitrator is notified to the parties is for him, the arbitrator, to convene the preliminary meeting (see Chapter 4, page 21). At that meeting the arbitrator will give directions for delivery of statements of case and of defence unless such directions are given (as in the present case) by the rules prescribed by the agreement. See in this connection the provision made by the rules of the Chartered Institute of Arbitrators (1988 edition), Article 6; and of the London Court of International Arbitration (1985 edition), Article 6. The next step then is for delivery of the statement of case.

The statement of case

ARBITRATION UNDER THE RULES OF THE
LONDON COURT OF ARBITRATION *(1978 Edition)*

Z
of France

v.

CD Limited

———

STATEMENT OF CASE
on behalf of Z

1. Mr Z has invoked the arbitration clause, clause 13, of the fixed term Agreement concluded between Z and CD, a company incorporated and existing under the laws of England, having its registered office at London, on 9th January 1980, which came into effect on 1st September 1979 to expire on 31st August 1981 ('Agreement').

2. Z is an internationally known and experienced engineer who acts as an independent consultant in relation to the engineering and construction industry on a world-wide basis. Z had been known to CD for some time prior to the coming into effect of the Agreement.

3. CD, in its own words (see CD letter of 2nd May 1980 to Z), was 'established in 1978 to involve ourselves in projects in which the risks would be matched by good financial returns and in which the markets,

technologies and expertise, both inside and outside CD's product capability, would be explored and developed'.

4. The purpose of the engagement by CD of Z under the Agreement was *inter alia* as stated in clause 1 thereof to widen the areas where the influence of CD could be extended and to improve the ability of CD to bid for complete turnkey projects.

5. The duties of Z under the Agreement were stated in clause 2 thereof to include in particular the following:

'(a)   The publicising of CD and promoting its potential to undertake projects in the engineering field with persons and concerns in Continental Europe and other areas to be agreed;

(b)   The providing of a good liaison with customers after contracts relating to projects have been entered into;

(c)   The assistance of CD in the obtaining of payment under such contracts.'

6. Z had on 1st August 1979 entered into an agreement with PQ, an entity established and existing under the laws of Liechtenstein whose registered office is Vaduz, Liechtenstein whereby he made his services available to PQ but not on an exclusive basis.

7. PQ entered into an agreement dated 10th October 1979, but effective from 1st September 1979, with RS, a company incorporated and existing under the laws of Panama, whose registered office is Panama City, Panama whereby PQ agreed and undertook to make available to RS the services of Z for the following purposes for an indefinite period commencing on 1st September 1979:

'(a)   To bring to the attention of and to introduce to major engineering and construction companies turnkey projects in the engineering field on a worldwide basis;

(b)   To provide assistance to such companies in the negotiation of any and all contracts relating to such projects.'

8. Under this agreement (clause 3) RS had the right to give specific instructions to Z regarding which companies were to be the subject at any given time of the services referred to in the clauses quoted in the preceding paragraph.

9. Moreover, under this agreement RS had the right to instruct Z:

'(a)   In the performance of his services as referred to in clause 2 above not to propose terms or price to any potential customers or any of the companies falling within the scope of clause 3 above without the prior written approval of a duly authorised officer of any such company;

(b)   Not to disclose to any third party any information which he may acquire concerning any such company.'

10. RS concluded a fixed term Agreement with CD ('RS Agreement') on 9th January 1980 which was stated to commence on 15th October 1979 and to expire on 31st August 1981 but was effective from 1st September 1979. Under the RS Agreement, RS made available to CD the services of Z for the following purposes:

'2.   (a)   To bring to the attention of and to introduce to CD turnkey projects in the engineering field on a worldwide basis ('projects');

(b)   To provide assistance to CD in the negotiation of contracts relating to projects.'

11. The Agreement together with the RS Agreement which was complementary thereto and recognised as such by the parties (see CD letter to RS of 2nd May 1980) replaced a letter contract dated 30th May 1979 which was signed on behalf of CD and accepted by Z. This contract contained substantially similar clauses to those in the Agreement and in the RS Agreement. Notably it provided that Z should 'work full time for CD' and that he should receive 'an all-in fee of £   per annum'.

12. With reference to the total annual gross fee of £   payable by CD under the Agreement and under the RS Agreement, Z had earned in excess of this level of remuneration in direct salary and benefits over each of the three years immediately preceding 1st September 1979.

13. From 1st September 1979 until CD unlawfully and retroactively terminated the Agreement with effect from 1st May 1980 by its letter of 2nd May 1980 which letter was modified in one respect by CD's letter of 22nd May 1980, Z fully and continuously performed his duties

under the Agreement. CD instructed Z to undertake work of other CD Group companies. Z undertook the activities on behalf of CD and other companies in the CD Group during the period concerned as set out in his Affidavit sworn 23rd September 1980 delivered herewith. It will be seen from this that Z was constantly and continuously active during the period concerned.

14. Z was involved in numerous specific potential projects which he identified and/or followed during the period from 1st September 1979 to 30th April 1980 (see Affidavit delivered herewith). Z took the first substantial move on behalf of any CD Group company in relation to about 90% of these potential projects.

15. It follows from the considerations mentioned in paras. 13 and 14 above that Z fully and continuously performed his duties under the Agreement. He even established an office in France 15 minutes from Geneva Airport at the request of CD. CD has accepted that Z fully and continuously performed his duties under the Agreement by virtue of having reimbursed him for all the expenses incurred by him in relation to his activities as described in Affidavit No. 6 delivered herewith. Moreover, CD in its letter of 2nd May 1980 to Z made no suggestion that he had not fully performed his obligations under the Agreement. CD must now be considered as estopped from denying this.

16. The reasons for the unlawful termination and consequential breach of the Agreement by CD were set out in its letter of 2nd May 1980 (see document delivered herewith). It is clear from the terms of this letter that the breach of the Agreement by CD was based solely upon a fundamental change in CD Group policy. CD's letter specifically stated that this fundamental change in CD Group policy had made Z 'along with CD's other outside consultants, an inevitable casualty'. It is further relevant to state that CD had closed its operating offices. CD made most of its own staff redundant. CD considerably diminished its operations in relation to potential projects outside the United Kingdom. These moves took place only two years after CD was established. No experienced international company could expect, by the very nature of the business, to be able to achieve satisfactory results within such a brief period of time.

17. 1st May 1980 was the date from which CD by its unlawful termination of the Agreement and consequential breach thereof ceased to make it possible for Z to perform fully his obligations under the Agreement. However, Z is willing and in a position to continue to perform fully his obligations under the Agreement until the date of the expiration of the Agreement, namely 31st August 1981. Z had been asked by CD by a letter of 18th March 1980 (document delivered herewith) not to undertake any 'overseas journey or direct action on behalf of the company' pending further instructions. This letter, however, was to this effect only.

18. CD was asked on behalf of Z to withdraw by 14th June 1980 its letter of 2nd May 1980 but refused to do so. Consequently, as from 15th June 1980 Z approached other potentially interested organisations without prejudice to his position as stated in the preceding paragraph, having regard to the doctrine of mitigation.

19. Document No. 8 delivered herewith lists the organisations which have been approached with date of approach and summary of the responses received. Where there is no summary this means that no response has been received. None of the approaches have led to offers of suitable employment for Z. Similar negative responses are to be expected from other international organisations. Evidence of this is to be found in CD's own letter of 2nd May 1980 (document No. 2) where it is stated, *inter alia*:

' . . . Also, as you will be aware, the present industrial climate is not favourable to the contracting industry and we, like others, are having to structure our organisation accordingly in order to reduce costs.'

Since CD wrote those words on 2nd May 1980 the world economic climate has continued to deteriorate. This has meant that organisations which might have considered engaging Z in better times will not be in a position to do so for at least a further twelve months.

20. It follows that until the expiration date of the Agreement it is highly likely that neither Z (not RS acting in relation to Z) will be able to find suitable employment for Z within his specialist field.

21. Assuming that there is a duty to try to mitigate in the present case,

this duty has been fulfilled by Z. Provided it is fulfilled, if the results are nil, no allowance for mitigation can be made in the amount of damages due for breach of contract.

22. There are two claims.

Primary claim: £   by way of damages for breach of the Agreement

23. CD has terminated the Agreement without having legal grounds to do so and therefore unlawfully. CD has accordingly 'breached the contract'. It follows that CD is liable to Z in damages.

24. In this type of case, 'prima facie, the measure of damages for wrongful dismissal is the amount which 'the employee' would have received if the employment had continued in accordance with contract . . .' (see *Halsbury's Laws of England*, Fourth Edition, Volume 12, para. 1178). Although Z was acting as an independent consultant under the Agreement the above-quoted measure of damages applies by analogy. A duty to try to mitigate lies upon Z but the other employment which he can take must be both suitable and available (see ibid.). But where this duty has been fulfilled and the results are nil no allowance for mitigation can be made in the computation of damages due for breach of contract (see para. 21 above).

25. It follows from the considerations in the preceding paragraph that as a further £   is due to Z under the terms of the Agreement (see para. 34 below) that is the measure of normal damages and forms the first element in this primary claim.

26. However, in this case there is a second element forming part of the primary claim. This is the damage caused to Z by the particular circumstances resulting from the unlawful action by CD. Whilst Z does not claim additional damages for his injured feelings, he is entitled to additional damages to his credit and/or reputation since such injury must have been within the presumed contemplation of the parties as a likely result of the breach (see *Halsbury's* op.cit., para. 1188).

27. The reason why Z was engaged by CD under the Agreement was his record as a first-class engineer highly familiar with the negotiation and implementation of large international engineering and construction contracts. Evidence of this is to be found in Z's curriculum vitae covering the years 1963–1979 (document No. 10).

28. By virtue of his record and extensive experience Z had become very well known and respected in the international engineering and construction business. It was precisely because of this that his duties under the Agreement were stated in clause 2(a) to include:

'The publicising of CD and promoting its potential to undertake projects in the engineering fields with persons and concerns in Continental Europe and other areas to be agreed.'

29. It follows that CD was fully aware of Z's international credit and reputation when it entered into the Agreement.

30. The fact of CD's termination of the Agreement has become general knowledge in the international construction and engineering business partly because the absence of Z as a specialist in his field from the normal circuit, which he frequented on behalf of CD from 1st September 1979 until breach, has become noticed by those concerned in the international industry, and partly because of his own new approaches to organisations which believed that he was fully committed until 1st September 1981. Despite the fact that the breach has been admitted by CD to have been caused solely by a fundamental change in CD Group policy (see para. 16 above), nevertheless other executives, companies, groups and governments may well believe that other reasons were the cause of CD's unlawful termination and breach.

31. It follows that Z has suffered injury to his international credit and/or reputation by reason of CD's breach and is therefore entitled to additional damages on this account. The measure of such damages is equivalent to the amount which CD contracted to pay by way of fees for one year under the Agreement and under the RS Agreement, namely £   .

32. Accordingly, the total amount under the primary claim is £ (see para. 25 above) and £   (see para. 31 above), namely an overall total of £_____ .

Secondary claim: £   as a contractual debt due by CD to Z

33. CD terminated the Agreement without any legal ground whatsoever. CD did not seek a legal justification for its unlawful termination and breach of the Agreement since one could not be found. CD has

offered Z £15,000 as a so-called 'final settlement' (see document No. 5).

34. Under the Agreement Z was entitled to receive £   over the fixed two-year term. As of 1st May 1980, in effect, £   had been paid by CD to Z (of which £   was actually paid about 10th May 1980). Therefore a further £   is due by CD to Z by way of contractual debt.

35. Z has not elected to rescind the Agreement as a result of CD's unlawful breach thereof. Z remains able and willing to perform his obligations under the Agreement. For these reasons Z is entitled to the sum of £   , with interest at current market rates on each quarterly instalment which is paid to Z after the date when it would otherwise have become due (see 'suggested schedule of invoices' dated 4th January 1980 which was mutually agreed between the parties, document No. 9).

36. The claim under this heading is therefore £_____ as a contractual debt with interest as stated in para. 35 above.

Summary of substantive claims
37. Z prays for the following awards:

   (a) An award of £_____ by way of damages for breach of the Agreement (see para. 32 above);
   (b) An award of £_____ by way of contractual debt (see para. 36 above).

Claim for costs under Rule 15 of the Court
38. Z prays that:
   (a) His costs of the arbitration shall be payable by CD.
   (b) The costs of the award shall be payable by CD.

(signed) Counsel for the Claimant

....

on behalf of Z

1st October 1980

LIST OF DOCUMENTS

No.	Date	Title
1	9th January 1980	Agreement signed by CD and Z.
2	2nd May 1980	Letter from CD to Z.
3	9th January 1980	Agreement between CD and RS.
4	30th May 1980	Letter contract signed on behalf of CD and accepted by Z as stated in his letter of 9th June 1979.
5	22nd May 1980	Letter from CD to Z.
6	23rd September 1980	Affidavit by Z relating to his activities on behalf of CD and other companies in the CD Group starting from the first day of September 1979 until 16th May 1980.
7	23rd September 1980	Affidavit by Z listing projects with which he was involved on behalf of CD and other companies in the CD Group starting from the first day of September 1979 until May 1980.
8	23rd September 1980	Affidavit by Z listing the organisations which have been approached as from 15th June 1980 for the purposes of securing suitable employment for Z.
9	4th January 1980	Suggested schedule of invoices.
10	23rd September 1980	Z: curriculum vitae 1963–1979.
11	1st August 1979	Agreement between PQ and Z.
12	10th October 1979	Agreement between PQ and RS.
13	9th January 1980	Letter of understandings signed on behalf of CD and Z.
14	2nd May 1980	Letter from CD to RS.
15	18th March 1980	Letter from CD to Z.

Note: It will be observed from the above statement of case that, although the arbitration was commenced between Z and CD Limited as the parties to the agreement of 9th January 1980, the claim disclosed by the statement is made on behalf of RS as well as Z, as agreed by all parties. Accordingly, the statement of defence delivered on behalf of the respondent, CD, makes this clear by including RS in the title as 'Second Claimant', by agreement of the parties and approval of the arbitrator, and took the following form.

The statement of defence

ARBITRATION UNDER THE RULES OF THE LONDON
COURT OF ARBITRATION (1978 Edition)

Between

Z	<u>First Claimant</u>
AND	
RS	<u>Second Claimant</u>
AND	
CD Limited	<u>Respondents</u>

STATEMENT OF DEFENCE

1. It is admitted that:

   (i) The First Claimant entered into an agreement in writing dated 9th January 1980 with the Respondents; and

   (ii) The Second Claimant entered into a separate agreement in writing also dated 9th January 1980 with the Respondents.

2. The Respondents will refer to the said agreements at the hearing of this Arbitration for their full terms, meaning and effect.

3. The Respondents further admit their letters dated 2nd May 1980 which were addressed respectively to the First and Second Claimants. By the terms of those letters the said agreements were terminated with effect from 1st May 1980. The Respondents will refer to the letters on the hearing of this Arbitration for their full terms, meaning and effect.

4. The Respondents contend that the said agreements are now at an end.

PARTICULARS

(i)   The Respondents will rely on the letters of 2nd May 1980; and/or alternatively

(ii) The Respondents will contend that by their commencement of this Arbitration and/or by reason of the facts and matters pleaded by the Claimants in their respective Statements of Case the Claimants have accepted that the said agreements are at an end.

5. The Respondents deny that the Claimants or either of them have suffered the alleged or any loss or damage claimed or that there is due and owing to the Claimants or either of them any sum of money either as claimed or at all. The Claimants are, in any event, put to strict proof of such claims.

6. Save as aforesaid each and every allegation contained in the respective Statements of Case is denied and the Respondents deny that they are liable to the Claimants as alleged or at all.

(signed) Counsel for the Respondents

....

Dated the 19th day of November 1980.

Note: It will be seen that this is a simple defence, putting the claimants to strict proof of their claim, and that no counterclaim by the respondents is made. Had there been such a counterclaim, or if for other reasons the claimants felt that a reply to the defence was necessary or desirable, such a reply (and defence to counterclaim) would now be delivered, as provided by the rules under which the arbitration was being conducted.

The preliminary meeting

Following the closure of pleadings – in a case administered by the Court – the time has come for the preliminary meeting to be convened by the arbitrator. Where the arbitration is not so administered, but is in the hands of the arbitrator himself, the meeting will have been convened by him soon after acceptance of appointment – see page 130 above – at which he will give directions for delivery of pleadings as well as those relating to the further conduct of the arbitration. At the preliminary meeting discussion will ensue concerning discovery, representation, evidence and arrangements for the hearing, as illustrated by the orders of directions made by the arbitrator in the present case.

Order of directions (no. 1)

IN THE LONDON COURT OF ARBITRATION
IN THE MATTER OF THE ARBITRATION ACTS 1950 to
1979

and

IN THE MATTER OF AN ARBITRATION UNDER THE RULES
OF THE LONDON COURT OF ARBITRATION (1978 Edition)

BETWEEN	Z and RS	<u>Claimants</u>
AND	CD Limited	<u>Respondent</u>

WHEREAS I John Francis Phillips the sole arbitrator appointed in the above matter on the 19th November 1980

having (1) accepted such appointment on the 24th November 1980

(2) declared the closure of exchange of statements on the 17th December 1980

(3) heard the respective solicitors for the parties at a preliminary meeting on the 16th January 1981

NOW I HEREBY GIVE DIRECTIONS AS FOLLOWS:

1. The hearing of the arbitration will begin on the 5th day of March 1981 at 10.30 a.m. at the London Court of Arbitration at 75 Cannon Street, London EC4, subject to confirmation by the parties by 31st January 1981.

2.   The parties will be represented at the hearing by their respective solicitors and if they think fit by Counsel.

3.   There shall be discovery of documents between the parties by exchange of lists of documents and the production, inspection and supply of copies of documents in their respective possession relevant to this arbitration, such discovery to be completed by 20th February 1981; and after such discovery is completed, a bundle of such relevant documents including correspondence shall be prepared and agreed between the parties for their reference and that of the Arbitrator and shall be delivered to the Court by not later than the 25th February 1981.

4.   Evidence of the parties and their witnesses (which may include the evidence of Mr M and Mr N on behalf of the Claimants and Mr O and an expert witness on behalf of the Respondent) at the hearing of the arbitration is to be given orally on oath or affirmation provided that the evidence to be given by Mr M on behalf of the Claimants may be given by affidavit subject to the attendance of that witness at the hearing for cross-examination if required by the Respondent or the Arbitrator.

5.   Either of the parties on notice to the other is at liberty to apply to the Arbitrator for further directions.

6.   The costs of this order are to be costs in the reference.

Given under my hand in London the 22nd day of January 1981

....

Arbitrator

In the presence of

(signed) ....
Deputy Registrar

Note: In fact it is rarely possible for the case to proceed to the hearing as quickly and easily as is contemplated by the directions given above. In the present case, it was found that it would not be possible to undertake the hearing on 5th March 1981. The parties applied (under the 'liberty' given by the above order of directions) by correspondence for further directions, in consequence of which there was issued – by post, following telephone discussions between the parties' solicitors and the arbitrator – the following.

Order of directions (no. 2)

(1) The hearing of this arbitration will commence on Wednesday 1st April 1981 at 10.30 a.m. at the London Court of Arbitration at 75 Cannon Street, London EC4 and will continue until close of business on that day. If not by then concluded, the hearing will be adjourned until 2.30 p.m. on Friday 3rd April at the same place when the hearing shall continue until close of business on that day (unless earlier concluded). If not then completed, the hearing shall again be adjourned and resumed at a time and place to be agreed or fixed.

(2) Costs of the Application to be Costs in the Reference.

(3) Liberty to the Parties to Apply.

Interlocutory proceedings

Between the preliminary meeting and the hearing of the arbitration, there will often be interlocutory applications made by either or both parties for directions other than those illustrated above by the orders no. 1 and no. 2. Thus, following delivery of the statement of case (or defence) by one party, the other may apply (by 'restoring' the preliminary meeting) for directions requiring 'further and better particulars' to be given of the pleading in question, so that the issues dividing the parties may be refined, narrowed and made more precise. A party may also – with ostensibly the same objective – apply for leave to administer interrogatories. These are questions to be asked of the other party to elucidate his case and the contentions on which it is based – but will not be allowed by the arbitrator where the purpose is to 'fish' for evidence adverse to the applicant's case.

There may also be interlocutory applications for leave to amend pleadings. This may happen where, for instance, further and better particulars of a pleading have been given, rendering it desirable that the reply to that pleading is amended to take account of the further matters pleaded by the particulars. Since the procedure in arbitration is less formal than in litigation, leave to amend pleadings is very readily granted.

But there are other interlocutory applications which must be considered much more formally, and decided according to the *lex fori* – the law of the place in which the case is being tried. These include the application for security for costs. Where, for example, one of the parties is out of the jurisdiction and/or with limited assets within it, the other party may well apply (to the arbitrator, if the rules under which the arbitration is proceeding permit, or to the court) for security to be given for the applicant's costs by payment into court or by deposit in the joint names of the solicitors involved or in the name of the arbitrator. Indeed, the arbitrator may himself require that security be given in appropriate circumstances by either or both parties in respect of his own fees and expenses. Such applications, whether considered by the arbitrator or the court, are decided on the strict basis laid down by the *lex fori*, and in particular the Rules and Orders of the Supreme Court.

So also with applications designed to bring pressure to bear upon a party to proceed promptly towards the hearing; as in litigation where a defendant, frustrated by the dilatory conduct of the plaintiff, seeks an order for dismissal of the action for want of prosecution; or a plaintiff, similarly frustrated, seeks judgment in default of appearance or of defence.

In arbitration, where by definition the procedure is by choice and consent of the parties, the correct course for a claimant or respondent suffering such frustration and seeking finality is to apply to the arbitrator for a peremptory order requiring the party in default to remedy the default within a limited, reasonable and specified time, after which, so long as the arbitrator has secured such evidence as is possible of the fact that the defaulting party had full notice of the application and order, he may allow the case to go to hearing at the instance of the applicant.

But, when all the interlocutory proceedings are settled and the directions complied with, we come to the hearing and to the award – fully discussed in Chapter 5. In the present case the award took the following form.

The award

IN THE LONDON COURT OF ARBITRATION
IN THE MATTER OF THE ARBITRATION ACTS 1950 to 1979

AND

IN THE MATTER OF AN ARBITRATION UNDER THE RULES OF THE
LONDON COURT OF ARBITRATION (1978 Edition)

| BETWEEN | Z and RS | <u>Claimants</u> |
| AND | CD Limited | <u>Respondent</u> |

FINAL AWARD

WHEREAS

1. By an agreement ('the X agreement') dated 9th January 1980 made
between the Respondent of the one part and the Claimants of the
other part the Claimants warranted that they had secured the services
of Mr Z under a contract of indefinite duration which became effective
on 1st September 1979; and agreed and undertook to make available
to the Respondent the services of Mr Z outside the United Kingdom for
a period commencing on 1st September 1979 and ending on 31st
August 1981.

2. By an agreement ('the Y agreement') also dated 9th January 1980
made between the Respondent of the one part and Mr Z of the other
part Mr Z was engaged by the Respondent for a fixed period from 1st
September 1979 to 31st August 1981 as an independent consultant to
assist the Respondent in widening the areas where its influence could

be extended and in improving its ability to bid for complete turnkey projects, particular aspects of the duties of Mr Z under the agreement being set out therein.

3. By two letters both dated 2nd May 1980 the Respondent purported to give notice to the Claimants and to Mr Z of termination of both the X agreement and the Y agreement with effect from 1st May 1980.

4. The Claimants claim damages for breach of the X agreement and dispute the amount of compensation for termination offered by the Respondent in the said letter dated 2nd May 1980 as modified by a further letter from the Respondent to the Claimants of 22nd May 1980.

5. By clause 11 of the X agreement its validity construction and performance shall be governed by the law of England.

6. By clause 12 of the X agreement all disputes arising out of or in connection with the agreement including its validity construction and performance are to be determined by a sole Arbitrator appointed under the Rules of the London Court of Arbitration.

7. The Respondent has given notice to me in accordance with the provisions of s. 1(6)(a) of the Arbitration Act 1979 that a reasoned award would be required.

AND whereas it is convenient for and was agreed by the parties that any award of damages in respect of breach by the Respondents of the X agreement and the Y agreement should be calculated as a whole covering both agreements and thereafter divided in the proportions of two-thirds applicable to the X agreement and one-third to the Y agreement.

Now I, John Francis Phillips (a) having been appointed sole arbitrator in this matter on 18th November 1980; (b) having accepted such appointment on 24th November 1980; and (c) having heard and duly weighed the several submissions and arguments of the parties and of Counsel on their behalf and the evidence adduced, do Hereby make and publish this my AWARD in final settlement of all matters arising in this reference in manner following, that is to say:

1. I Find

(a) that the Respondent terminated the X agreement and the Y agreement as from 1st May 1980 without lawful excuse or justification.

(b) that the Claimants in the case of both the agreements elected to treat the agreements as at an end, consequent upon such unlawful termination and to rely for relief upon their respective claims for damages therefor.

(c) that the claims for damages may conveniently be dealt with under three heads viz. (i) contractual damages, (ii) damage to Mr Z's reputation and (iii) contract commission.

(d) as to 'contractual damages', that the Claimants are entitled (i) to payment in full of the amounts payable to them respectively by instalments as provided by the agreements from 1st May 1980 to 31st August 1981, namely £   and £   .

(ii) to interest at the agreed rate of 15% per annum on each instalment as from the dates agreed by the parties for payment of such instalments down to the date of this Award viz. 1st April 1981, such interest totalling £   .

(iii) there must be offset against such interest a discount representing interest upon instalments notionally paid in advance by their embodiment in the amount of this award, a deduction of £   resulting in a net figure of £   .

(iv) proper allowance must be made against the net total under (i), (ii) and (iii) above in respect of mitigation of loss which the Claimants achieved or are bound by law to achieve as far as is in the circumstances reasonable and practicable.

(v) in pursuance of such mitigation Mr Z did secure payment of a sum of US$ (converted at an agreed rate of £ sterling); but that no other deduction falls to be made in respect of mitigation since I find as a fact that in spite of all reasonable and proper efforts on the part of the Claimants no other income has been received or is likely to be received before 31st August 1981 resulting from the provision or performance of services by Mr Z; in particular I find as a fact that it was reasonably necessary for Mr Z to maintain the office and (until   ) secretarial staff which he had established at   for the purpose of fulfilling the agreements, so that no deduction by way of mitigation falls to be made in respect of economies which might have been made in that respect or any other relevant area.

(vi) the net amount payable in respect of 'contractual damages' therefore is £   less £   , namely £   .

(e) as to damage to Mr Z's reputation, I find that it was clear and known to all parties concerned that the termination of the agreements by the Respondent was due to a commercial decision deriving from world economic conditions affecting business in the relevant area, and was not intended to, nor did, reflect adversely upon Mr Z's high standing and reputation. Nor is there any evidence whatever that the decision of the Respondent did have the effect of damaging Mr Z's reputation. Moreover, had it been necessary to do so I would have held as a matter of law that no claim for such damages would lie in such a case as this; and I award nothing in respect of this head of claim for damages.

(f) as to contract commission, referred to in clauses 3(b) and 4 of the X agreement, I find that no contracts have been entered into by the Respondent resulting from the performance of the services of Mr Z under the agreements and that no such contracts are reasonably likely so to be entered into by the Respondent whether before or after 31st August 1981; and that therefore no sum by way of contract commission is payable in fact or in law, and that nothing is to be awarded in respect of this head of claim for damages.

AND I AWARD AND ADJUDGE

1. That the Respondent do pay to the Claimant Z the sum of £   by way of damages for unlawful termination of the X agreement, representing two-thirds of the total damages payable in respect of termination of both the X and the Y agreements.

2. That the Respondent do pay the costs of this Award which I tax and settle at the sum of £   (including my fees and charges in the sum of £   ); provided that if the Claimants shall in the first instance

have paid the costs of this Award they shall be entitled to immediate reimbursement from the Respondent of the sum so paid.

3. That the Respondent do pay to the Claimants their costs of this reference to be taxed unless agreed and do bear his own costs of this reference.

4. Fit for Counsel.

In witness whereof I have hereunto set my hand this   day of April 1981.

Signed and published

....

Arbitrator

(signed) ....
Witness

Index

award *(continued)*
  interest on, 31, 32
  interim, 29, 68
  judicial review of, 13, 85
  jurisdiction, 13
  preparation of, 28, 46
  publication of, 27, 30
  purpose of, 28
  reasons for, 13, 29, 46
  register of, 32
  remit, 13
  set aside, 13, 70, 71

Baltic Exchange, 20
bias, arbitrator of, 22
Bremer Vulkan case, 17
British Telecom, 5

case stated, 13
Chartered Institute of Arbitrators, 5, 18, 19, 20, 21, 36, 53, 54
  rules of, 19, 51, 52, 93 *et seq.*
chartered secretaries, 3
Citizens' Advice Bureau, 5
Civil Evidence Act, 25
conciliation, 7, 8
construction industry, 20
contracts
  international, 11 *et seq.*
  proper law of, 35
costs
  application for, 25
  award of, 30, 69, 106, 115
  directions for, 25, 99
  documents only, of, 56
  generally, 30, 69
  hearing, of, 26, 27
  payment of, 31
  procedure, of, 43
  reasonable, 30
  reference, of, 30
  security for, 17
  taxation of, 14, 30, 31, 70
  tribunal of, 107
directions
  order of precedents, 145 *et seq.*
discovery, 24
documents
  arbitration, 52, 53, 54, 55, 58
  court, in, 17, 96
  disclosure, 24
  inspection of, 24
  list of precedent, 140
  submission of, 103
  supply of, 24, 118
documents-only arbitration

appeal, 57
costs, 55
enforcement, 57
generally, 55 *et seq.*
procedure, 54 *et seq.*

European Community, 37
evidence
  Civil Evidence Act, 25
  documents, 17, 24
  expert, 17, 25, 45
  generally, 14, 15, 76, 77, 113
  hearing, procedure, 26, 27
  witnesses, 24, 25, 26, 66, 67, 97, 104, 119
expert witness, 17, 25, 45, 113

Grain and Feed Trade Association (GAFTA), 20

hearing, 26, 27, 45, 66, 97, 103, 113
High Court
  appeals to, 13, 33
  powers, 15
Holdsworth, 16

Institution of Civil Engineers, 20
interest, 30, 31
International Bar Association
  Supplementary Rules on Evidence in International Commercial Arbitration, 116 *et seq.*
International Chamber of Commerce (ICC), 19, 35
Court of Arbitration, 19
interrogatories, 17
  Ius Gentium, 9, 10

judges, 17
judgment in default, 17
judicial review, 13, 14
judicial systems
  adversarial, 16
  inquisitorial, 17

Law Centres, 5
lex fori, 12, 13
Lloyd's, 20
London Chamber of Arbitration, 18
London Court of International Arbitration (LCIA), 12, 18, 20, 21, 35
  rules of, 100 *et seq.*
London Maritime Arbitrators' Association, 20

mediation, 78
merchants' courts, 3